Kriegie

★ ★ ★

KRIEGIE

An American POW in Germany

OSCAR G. RICHARD III

★ ★ ★

LOUISIANA STATE UNIVERSITY PRESS

BATON ROUGE

M M

Designer: Rebecca Lloyd Lemma
Typeface: Janson
Typesetter: Crane Composition, Inc.
Printer and binder: Thomson-Shore, Inc.

Library of Congress Cataloging-in-Publication Data:

Richard, Oscar.
    Kriegie : an American POW in Germany / Oscar G. Richard, III.
        p. cm.
    Includes bibliographical references.
    ISBN 0–8071–2562–8 (cloth : alk. paper)
    1. Richard, Oscar. 2. World War, 1939–1945—Prisoners and prisons, German. 3. World War, 1939–1945—Personal narratives, American. 4. Prisoners of war—Germany—Biography. I. Title.

D805.G3 R46 2000
940.53'7243—dc21
                                                                99-088025

For my wife,
Billie,
who for many years
urged me to write this story

Contents

★　★　★

CONTENTS

Illustrations

★ ★ ★

Kriegie

Prologue

★　　★　　★

Americans born in the first third of this century have done more for their country and the world than any generation in history. They stood up to Hitler, Tojo, Mussolini and Stalin and their successors, met their challenges head on and relegated fascism, Nazism, Japanese militarism and Communism to the ashcan of history.

—STEPHEN E. AMBROSE[1]

I was born to that generation, exactly twenty years before the day Japan bombed Pearl Harbor and plunged our nation into the Second World War.

On the Sunday of December 7, 1941, my brother, two of my sisters, and I drove from our home in Sunshine, Louisiana, to Baton Rouge to celebrate my birthday. We were going to the Paramount Theater to see *Blues in the Night*, starring Bing Crosby. As we neared the theater that afternoon, we saw newsboys hawking an EXTRA edition of the *Morning Advocate*. Six-inch-high letters on the front page screamed WAR.

I was then in my senior year at Louisiana State University in Baton Rouge, but it was inevitable that I, like hundreds of thousands of others of my generation, would soon find myself in the United States armed services. Some of my classmates were drafted;

1. "How World War II Reshaped the American Future," *AARP Bulletin*, July-August 1995.

1

some enlisted. My draft number didn't come up during my final semester, but I knew it wouldn't be long before it did. I tried to enlist in the Marine Corps officer training school at Quantico, Virginia, but failed the physical examination. Still, I was determined to make my own choice of service. On the morning of commencement day at LSU (the ceremony was to be held that night), I rode a bus from the campus to Harding Field in Baton Rouge and enlisted as an aviation cadet in the U.S. Army Air Corps. I passed that physical. Unlike the Marine Corps, the army didn't believe a couple of missing teeth qualified as a physical disability.

The aviation cadet program had become so heavily enrolled, however, that I had to wait several months before being inducted. In the interim, I continued working at the university press, where I had been employed as a student worker my senior year.

Late fall 1942, I left the press for a job at the Golden Gate cane syrup mill, which my grandfather had founded some fifty years earlier. My job was to maintain the flow of cane juice into and out of a series of tanks. I worked shifts of six hours on, six hours off.

During the morning shift on November 27, 1942, my cousin Percy came running to the mill with a red-bordered envelope addressed to me. The War Department was ordering me to report to the army's district recruiting and induction office in New Orleans on December 7, my twenty-first birthday. The night before I was due to report, I stayed with my aunt and uncle who lived on Prytania Street in New Orleans. I went to the Orpheum Theater and watched a movie starring Errol Flynn and Ronald Reagan. The next day, I boarded a train with twenty-three other cadets from Louisiana, bound toward Los Angeles. From Los Angeles, we were shipped via the Pacific Electric Railway to nearby Santa Ana Army Air Base, headquarters for the army's west coast air training command and basic training facility.

Stateside

★ ★ ★

Santa Ana was picturesque, with the San Gabriel mountains to the northeast, the Pacific Ocean to the west, and citrus and eucalyptus trees everywhere else you looked. The site had drawbacks, though, such as torrential rains and the sandstorms kicked up by the Santa Ana winds. My introduction to Santa Ana and the service was chilling. A heavy fog had rolled in overnight from the Pacific, enshrouding the area. Earlier that morning, before I and my fellow Louisianans arrived, two cadets, blindly dashing toward barracks after roll call, had collided head-on. One died from the collision. As we pulled into the Santa Ana station, we could see his coffin being loaded onto an outbound train.

Santa Ana was a preflight classification and training center for aviation cadets—soon to be pilots, bombardiers, and navigators of the Army Air Force. Like most cadets, our days were filled with calisthenics, drill, classes, and lectures. We spent a week in psychological, manual, mental, and physical testing to determine whether we were best suited for training as a pilot, a bombardier, or navigator. But we soon learned that the current need of the air force was the determining factor for classification. Even though my testing qualified me for all three flight crew officer categories, I, along with most of my class, was selected for bombardier training.

Other training, testing, and activities at Santa Ana included sessions of gunnery, pressure chamber training, close order drill, and parades.

We were taken to the Pacific Ocean beach at nearby Newport to learn how to fire .45-caliber automatic pistols, carbines, rifles, and Thompson submachine guns, or "Tommy guns," like those used by gangsters in the 1930s.

The pressure chamber simulated atmospheric conditions at high altitudes, where lack of oxygen could result in diminishment of concentration, unconsciousness, and, if not corrected, death. The chamber was located on the current site of the John Wayne Airport in Orange County.

Our physical education instructors included such notables as Marty Brill, who had served as quarterback on the last team coached by Knute Rockne at Notre Dame; Tom Harmon, the great Heisman Trophy winner from the University of Michigan; John Kimbrough, All-American from Texas A & M; and Joe DiMaggio of the New York Yankees.

Every Sunday afternoon more than a thousand cadets suffered through dress parade. Nearly every time two or three cadets passed out, overcome by the blazing hot sun, which was exacerbated by hangovers resulting from weekend passes to Los Angeles.

Only upperclassmen, though, qualified for these coveted passes. As a cadet I spent my first Christmas Eve on guard duty—in the rain—and Christmas Day on KP. By New Year's Day I qualified for a pass and went to see the sights in Los Angeles and Hollywood, staying at the Biltmore Hotel, which was jammed each and every weekend with service men. That time the hotel's Biltmore Bowl featured Ozzie Nelson's band, with vocalist Harriet Hilliard and Ted Lewis of "Me and My Shadow" fame. I also visited the Hollywood Canteen, a USO establishment staffed by motion picture stars. On later trips to L.A. I toured the MGM, Paramount, and RKO movie studios, as well as the national radio network studios, where I saw the"Lux Radio Theater," produced by Cecil B. DeMille, and a variety show starring Al Jolson.

*　　*　　*

After a few weeks of preflight training at Santa Ana, I was sent to Victorville bombardier school. Located west of the San Gabriels on the edge of the Mojave Desert, Victorville, California, offered a different view and considerably different weather conditions from Santa Ana. In the distant southwest, Old Baldy still wore its snow cap, but in our barracks we had to use cooling to offset the desert heat. Boxes about the size of window air-conditioning units were filled with water-soaked excelsior and equipped with fans to draw and cool the dry desert air.

We soon realized that preflight training at Santa Ana was a snap compared to flight training at Victorville. Our day began with reveille at five-thirty in the morning and went nonstop until nine at night. Classes, both intensive and extensive, included calculus, trigonometry, ballistics, meteorology, cryptography, Morse code, physics, and physical education. The going joke was that if you dropped a pencil, by the time you reached to retrieve it, you might miss a whole semester.

We got an early introduction to the intricacies of the famed Norden bombsight, which at that time was classified top secret. The Norden Company originally manufactured the instrument for the U.S. Navy as a navigational device, but in 1933, it was acquired by the U.S. Army Air Corps, which had the company modify it for use as a precision bombsight. The Norden bombsight was reputed to be so accurate it enabled the dropping of a bomb into a pickle barrel from an altitude of five miles. Before we could view the top-secret device, bombardier cadets were subjected to security clearance by the Federal Bureau of Investigation. When we began flight training we were required to carry a .45-automatic pistol when checking out a bombsight from the vault where the devices were stored. The armed cadet would carry it in a canvas bag to and from the plane, an AT-11 twin-engine trainer. The sight never was left in the plane, and it always was kept covered when not in use.

I found out much later that these precautions had been fruitless. A citizen who had worked for the Norden Company had provided German intelligence with blueprints and had even traveled to Germany to give the Nazi experts further details.

In a letter home dated March 8, 1943, I wrote: ". . . We started right off on a full schedule today, beginning with five hours on the ground trainer, using the Norden sight. It's the most complex piece of machinery I've ever seen. It's amazing that anyone could devise such an instrument. There's so many switches and knobs and other gadgets on it that it almost drives you nuts just to look at it."

We first practiced using the sight on a ground trainer, a wheeled platform structure elevated about fifteen feet above the hangar floor. The platform had space for the sight, one cadet, and an instructor. The target was a printed paper bulls-eye mounted atop a moving wheeled box.

When we became more familiar with the bombsight, then we practiced from the trainer plane, dropping hundred-pound sand-filled missiles that contained gun powder to create a puff of smoke to mark their impact. Each flight training mission carried one instructor and two cadets. While one cadet sat in the plane's nose compartment with the instructor, the other was in the rear, filming the bomb's impact through a small aperture in the floor. The target was a pyramid-shaped pile of wood on the surface of the desert, around which several concentric circles were marked at one-hundred-foot intervals. We called the target a "shack." A direct hit was also termed a "shack." By studying the films, instructors could determine a cadet's score, or circular error. Cadets were quick to blame the pilot or a faulty gyroscope in the bombsight for an excessively high circular error, as a cadet with an unacceptably high cumulative error was subject to being "washed out," or dismissed from flight officer training and transferred to ground duty.

"Our ground school instructor says the real good bombardiers are just now getting into combat," I explained in a letter home to my folks. "They used to be enlisted men who were taught what to do on the bombsight, but who didn't know how the thing worked. A few months ago they were in need of a great many bombardiers and they put almost anybody through. But now they want quality bombardiers for precision bombing. . . . You should hear the instructors knock the British bombing. One of them said they haul a load of bombs in those Wellington bombers and say 'Okay, boys, we're over Germany now, dump 'em out!'"

We weren't as close to Hollywood at Victorville as we had been at Santa Ana, but we still had our stars. One of the officers was Tennessee Ernie Ford. And among the cadets were two film actors—Tim Holt and Robert Sterling. Holt, son of cowboy star Jack Holt, had appeared in *Hitler's Children* with Bonita Granville and in

The Treasure of the Sierra Madre with Humphrey Bogart and Walter Huston.

A few days before members of our class were graduated and commissioned second lieutenants, we had a party at the Beverly Wilshire Hotel at Rodeo Drive and Wilshire Boulevard in Los Angeles. Our guest for the occasion was Jack Carson, who had appeared in *The Strawberry Blonde* with Jimmy Cagney, Rita Hayworth, and Olivia de Havilland. Lavish parties for graduating cadets from Victorville were traditional and usually paid for by officers who were in the motion picture industry.

★　★　★

After being commissioned, I received orders to report to Army Air Force gunnery school at Kingman, Arizona. But when I reported there, along with a couple of other newly commissioned officers from Victorville, we were greeted with puzzled looks from the officers in charge. "You're not supposed to be here for another week," we were told. An unexpected week's leave—we weren't about to spend it in that forsaken Arizona desert town. We left on the next train to Los Angeles.

When I returned to Kingman I discovered that my fellow lieutenants and I were in the minority. Most of the men stationed there were sergeants, being trained to man machine guns on bomber crews. Some were ex-aviation cadets who had washed out.

At Kingman, we concentrated on developing our marksmanship, firing various weapons in varied situations: shotguns at clay pigeons on a skeet shooting range; .50-caliber machine guns, ground-to-ground, ground-to-air, and air-to-air. Also on the gunnery training menu were sessions with the ball turret and upper turret guns aimed by Sperry gunsight. We learned how to strip and reassemble the .50-caliber machine gun, then do it blindfolded. Compared to the Norden bombsight, the machine gun was the height of simplicity, but both were highly effective instruments at the time.

As at other bases, close order drill and weekly dress parades were part of the training ritual. The temperature was extremely hot during the day when we had to drill, but thankfully cooler at night. It was even hotter and drier at Yucca Flats, where we went for a

week-long session of air-to-air firing. With the humidity register-
ing near zero we could almost wash and rinse our underwear and
wave it outside to dry. We looked forward to showers and air-to-air
flights to temporarily escape the blazing heat.

Fortunately our stay there was short. I was soon on my way to
Ephrata, Washington, to train as a crew member for a B-17.

★   ★   ★

I first read about the B-17 in an article, "Flying Fortress," published in a late 1930s edition of the *Saturday Evening Post*. In glow-
ing terms the article described the new four-engine airplane
produced by the Boeing Company in Seattle, Washington. The B-17
had a wingspan of more than one hundred feet, weighed about seventeen tons, and had an airspeed of about 150 to 185 miles per
hour. Its cost—a mere fraction of today's air craft—$250,000.

The army and navy were skeptical of the B-17 when it first appeared and considered it only as an auxiliary to their other transport airplanes. In 1941 four of the originally designed B-17s were
sent to Great Britain, where the Royal Air Force tested them in
daytime combat over Germany. The results were far from encour-
aging. The English called them "flying targets." The Germans
called them "flying coffins."

But then the B-17 underwent modification, principally chang-
ing the shape of the tail fin, which originally was a tall, abruptly
vertical appendage. With the modification the tail became sloped
and faired into the upper rear of the fuselage, which not only made
the airplane appear more graceful, but made it more airworthy as
well.

In addition a later model, the B-17F, was designed to carry two
.50-caliber machine guns in the tail. A year after the U.S. Air Force
began flying the B-17s in England, a chin turret was installed below
the nose of the plane, which added more firepower against frontal
attacks. These two turret guns were operated by the crew's bombardier. The navigator, situated behind the bombardier in the back
part of the plexiglass nose, fired guns either side of the nose.

The most distinguishing and enduring characteristic of the B-17
was its hardiness in combat. Unsolicited letters came to the Boeing
company from pilots and crew members of B-17s telling stories of

the Fortress's incomparable ruggedness, which enabled them to continue flying even with severe raking over from German fighters and flak barrages. [1]

★ ★ ★

My first personal introduction to this famous bomber came shortly after I left Kingman and arrived at Ephrata Army Air Base in central Washington. There I also met my fellow crew members, and we began our first phase of transition training before assignment to duty.

Pilot Neil Britt of Lumberton, North Carolina, a graduate of the UNC Law School in Chapel Hill, was a gregarious talker, whose conversations were sprinkled with humorous colloquialisms.

Ray Haley, the copilot, was from Denver, Colorado. Ray's twin, Ralph, was also stationed at Ephrata, and we frequently had trouble telling these identical twins apart. They seemed to enjoy confusing us and sometimes would even substitute for one another in flight duty and other training chores. [2]

The navigator on our crew was Ernie Lindell, from nearby Grandview in southern Washington. On training flights we would occasionally "hedge hop" over the Lindell farm. Ernie said his Dad told him to "put a stop to these shenanigans. You guys have gotten the chickens so damned scared they've stopped layin' eggs and the cows are puttin' out buttermilk."

The engineer, Donald Tucker was from Kingston, New York. A quiet, no-nonsense kind of guy, Don was very able in carrying out his duties. In addition to helping keep the plane in good working order, Don manned the two machine guns in the top turret.

Morton Harris, Brooklyn, was the radio operator. He occupied

1. The B-17's fellow bomber, the B-24 Liberator, was bigger, faster, and could carry a heavier bomb load. The B-24 performed admirably in many of the major strikes during World War II, but it lacked the charisma of the Flying Fortress, mainly because of its appearance. Oversized and cumbersome compared to the B-17, it was known throughout the Eighth Air Force, particularly among the crews of the Fortresses, as "The Pregnant Cow." It also lacked the renowned ruggedness of its sibling.

2. Ray and Ralph occasionally dated the same woman, with the woman thinking she had only been dating one man.

the cubicle between the engineer's station and the bomb bay. Morton was a big man who loved to play the accordion.

Bill Argenbright from Louisville, Kentucky, joined the crew as ball turret gunner after the first was transferred to other duty. Bill was quiet and reserved. His position, curled up inside the revolving turret beneath the belly of the plane, was, in my opinion, the most dangerous.

The two waist gunners, stationed either side of the B-17's midsection, were both southerners: Morton Mason from Dublin, Georgia, and Conway Nichols from Birmingham, Alabama. Mason wore a perpetual grin and was probably the most humorous of the ten crew members. His companion gunner was pleasant, but more quiet.

Manning the tail guns was Clarence Wolfe, one of three westerners in the crew. He was from Del Mar, California, and said he had worked for Bing Crosby at his racetrack.

★ ★ ★

For our final training for air combat we were sent to Bend, Oregon. There we were joined with other B-17 bomber crewmen to form a provisional group. Unlike earlier crews, which moved intact as groups to combat areas, members of provisional groups were to serve as replacements for fliers who had completed a tour of duty or were lost in combat.

My stay at Bend was undoubtedly the best of my time in the Army Air Force. The fall weather was pleasant and the scenery spectacular. However, we did have two close calls.

The first occurred on a training mission. We were flying in tight formation and crept too close to the ship ahead and to our right. Only some quick thinking and maneuvering by Britt avoided a midair collision.

The second happened during a gunnery exercise off the coast of Oregon. While in flight we lost an engine and another was acting up. Rather than attempting to fly over the Three Sisters Mountains back to Bend Air Base, Britt began looking for a place to land west of the mountain range. He finally spotted an airstrip seemingly located in the middle of nowhere. There was no windsock visible, so Britt came down close to the strip. He had come in downwind, unfortunately, and quickly ran out of runway. Stationed in the nose section, I could see landing space disappearing, and I scrambled back to the area near the pilot and copilot station as the B-17 careered off the strip into a field of grain.

We walked to the nearest town, which happened to be Eugene, and called base headquarters to report our forced landing. They told us to stay put and said they would dispatch a truck to pick us up. We sat several hours at a diner somewhere in Eugene, eating, drinking coffee, flirting with the waitress, and generally cutting up before the truck finally arrived. The trip back through the mountains lasted until the wee hours of the next morning.

A couple of weeks later we completed training in the B-17 and were ready for assignment overseas. We were given a short leave to go home, made shorter by complicated schedules and routing. Transportation was a major problem because of wartime priorities. I boarded a bus to Portland for a flight home. From Portland, I flew on a commercial airline to Oakland, California, where I had to spend the night in the terminal waiting room sleeping on a bench. The next morning I went to Burbank, then took an early flight to Houston. At the Houston airport I was met by a USO volunteer, who invited me to spend the afternoon at the River Oaks Country Club near her home in the exclusive residential section of the city. After lunch and a swim she drove me to the Houston rail station for the last leg of the trip home. Four days for a trip that might take only a few hours today.

T w o

Shipping Out

★ ★ ★

During the few precious days leave at home before my assignment to active duty, I discovered that my cousin, Gerald
LaPlace, who had been reported missing in action a couple
weeks earlier, was then said to be a prisoner of war in Stalag 17.
This news, while putting a damper on my visit, was a relief to his
mother and father. Gerald was alive—and out of combat.

When my leave was over I had orders to report to a staging
area at Grand Island, Nebraska. It was late fall 1943 and Grand
Island seemed extremely cold to a Louisiana boy. Preparation for
shipping overseas didn't take long, so my crew and I spent our free
time attending a dance at a big hall in town, watching a high school
championship football game, and listening to a bombardier from
another crew play boogie-woogie on a piano in the officers club at
the base.

To make up for heavy war losses incurred during the latter part
of 1943, officials decided to split the crews to double the number of
planes being flown to England, half being flown by crew pilots and
half by pilots of the Air Transport Command. Thus Britt, Haley,
Lindell, Tucker and Harris flew over in one B-17. Argenbright,
Mason, Nichols, Wolfe, and I flew over in another piloted by the
ATC.

Taking advantage of the relatively light load in their plane,
Britt, Haley, and Lindell purchased as much bourbon and scotch as
they could find in Grand Island and loaded it in the ship's bomb

bay. How they managed to get it into our base in the English Midlands, I don't remember, but they did sell about half of it—at black market prices—to fliers who had tired of British stout and ale.

The plane I was in made several stops before going to England, the first at ATC headquarters at Dover Air Base near Wilmington, Delaware. With a full day layover, my crew and I took a train to nearby Philadelphia the morning after we arrived. Navy was playing the University of Pennsylvania football team that afternoon at Franklin Field. The game was sold out, and we didn't have tickets, but we managed to crash the gate to see the second half. After the game we spent some time at a nightclub called The Shangrila and barely got to the Philadelphia railroad station in time to catch the last train to Wilmington.

Next morning, for some inexplicable reason, our plane headed westward to Detroit. The following day we headed back east to Bangor, Maine, laying over for several hours at the base, where I was able to surprise Gordon LeBlanc, a friend from Saint Gabriel, Louisiana, with a visit. Our last stop before crossing the North Atlantic was Gander Air Field, as dreary a place as I've ever been. Located on the far eastern tip of Newfoundland, it was one of two airfields there that served as departure points to Europe. The other was located at Goose Bay. Gander's most distinctive feature was its single runway, which was wide enough for a small plane to land crossways.

★   ★   ★

The flight across the North Atlantic brought us the incredible sight of the Aurora Borealis, but the trip was arduous, and we were tired and hungry when we reached Nut's Corner in Northern Ireland and were reunited with the rest of our crew. After getting something to eat I went to my assigned quarters and slept soundly almost around the clock. From nearby Belfast we took a crowded ferry across the Irish Sea to the west coast of England. A train ride down through Liverpool took us to Bovington, where we received several days' instruction about the European theater of operations and ground training in flight, bombing, and gunnery simulators. Bovington was a sea of ankle-deep mud, not a blade of grass to be seen.

Finally in late November my crew was shipped to the 384th Bombardment Group at Grafton Underwood, near the town of Kettering. Ernie Lindell and I were assigned to a Nissen hut in Squadron 545, where I was shown a cot on which lay a bicycle, apparently left by an MIA. One of the men in the hut said, " You can have that bunk." Ernie reached into his B-4 bag and pulled out a bottle. "Anyone care for some scotch?" he asked. The occupants of the hut nearly fell over one another getting to the bottle. Our new roommates became friendlier after that.

We didn't stay in the 545th very long, however. Ray's twin, Ralph, had been assigned to the 547th, and Ray requested we be assigned there too. "We've been together since we've been in the army—through flight school, B-17 training, and now here," he said. Permission was granted.

The pages that follow could be the story of any one of some forty thousand or more members of the U.S. Eighth Air Force during nearly three years of combat in the skies over Europe during Word War II. My combat experience was limited to one week; that of a few even less and that of many much longer, depending on when they were involved in the air war and how lucky they were.

Grafton Underwood

★ ★ ★

The 384th Bombardment Group of the U.S. Army Eighth Air Force was located in the English Midlands near the village of Grafton Underwood, which we promptly nicknamed "Grafton Undermud." During that dreary winter we were stationed there the miserable goop was everywhere, and everyone at the station felt like giving the place back to the "Dookabaluke," the Duke of Buccleuch, on whose estate the base was situated.[1]

Grafton Underwood is located four miles east of Kettering on the road between Brigstock and Geddington. Its oldest building is the church of Saint James the Apostle, parts of which date back to the twelfth century. *Grafton* comes from the Old English *grafa*, grove, and tun, which means farm. *Underwood* was added to the name later because of the great many trees near the village.

The airfield was built in 1941 as a satellite field of the RAF base at neighboring Polebrooke, later home of the 351st Group.[2] When reverse lend-lease made British facilities available for American use, Grafton Underwood happened to be the first airfield available. Before the 384th moved there as a permanent tenant, the field was

1. I'm sure the Duke never really thought he had given his property to the Yanks— even temporarily. He and his chums would frequently ride around the property on horseback, right through the airfield, disregarding security as if it were peacetime. The officers in charge of the base never said anything.
2. Clark Gable flew several missions with the 351st while taking motion pictures of aerial combat for the Eighth Air Force.

occupied by four other American units: the 15th Bomb Squadron, the 97th Bomb Group, the 305th Bomb Group, and the 96th Bomb Group. The 384th arrived in England in late May of 1943.[3]

By late 1943 there were about 130 air bases clustered in an area north and northwest of London approximating the size of Vermont. The Eighth Air Force occupied much of this area, with forty-five bases accommodating heavy bombardment groups of B-17s and B-24s. Sixteen bases were occupied by the Eighth's escort fighter planes. Medium bombers of the Ninth Air Force and the British Royal Air Force bombers and fighters also crowded into this section of East Anglia.

Moreover, airfields in England were established in populated areas, which were steeped in history and whose landscape featured spires of churches and cathedrals. Accommodating the villages and towns and plots of farmland, air strips were laid out in as unobtrusive a fashion as possible. Adjacent structures were situated so as to interfere minimally in the lives and livelihoods of the temporary hosts.[4]

By contrast the airfields where we had trained in the United States generally were located in isolated areas on land suited only for airfields and bombing and gunnery ranges. The authors of *One Last Look*, Philip Kaplan and Rex Smith, described these areas as what troops in the Pacific called the *boondocks*, or *boonies*, a corruption of the word *bundok*, used by the Filipinos to describe places ". . . dismally distant from the comforts and temptations of civilized life. . . ."[5]

3. The 384th was formed December 1, 1942, at Gowen Field in Idaho and began a three-month training period at Wendover, Utah, on January 2, 1943. From there, the group went to Sioux City, Iowa, for its final phase of training before heading to England.
4. In spite of the oft-quoted complaint of the British males—"over-paid, over-sexed, and over here"—there developed a genuine bond of friendship between the Americans and the British, particularly with the children. The back yard of the Bland family home abutted the fringe of the 384th airfield. Young Quentin Bland loved to go through the hedge adjoining the base and gather bits and pieces of the paraphernalia of war. He was intrigued by his Yank neighbors, and his interest in them has continued for more than fifty-five years. A few years ago, Quentin told my son Reed, who was visiting England, that he was writing a history of the 384th and showed him some facts and figures about bombing missions I had flown.
5. One exception, in my experience, was the Santa Ana Air Base, headquarters for the West Coast Training Command. It was located in Orange County, only forty miles south of Los Angeles, in a relatively well-populated area reputed to be the wealthiest in the United States.

The proximity of the bases in Britain made it difficult for pilots returning from missions to locate their home fields. Alternatively, when a plane came back to England disabled or nearly out of fuel, the pilot could always find a place to land.

The principal problem created by the crowding of airfields was experienced at the onset of missions, when all the bombers would have to assemble in combat formation before leaving the coast. Early on, leaders of the Eighth Air Force realized this would be necessary. Just across the Channel, Nazi fighters were poised to pounce on any small or loosely formed group of planes, and by assembling in tight, three-tiered formations, the heavily armed bombers could maximally protect themselves from assault.[6] And climbing to altitude while still over England provided at least some protection against the dreaded flak waiting a few miles away.[7] In reality, though, there was little defense against flak.[8]

The congestion caused by the planes assembling in combat formation in such limited airspace was hazardous. Within a ten-mile radius there might be four or five groups, each consisting of twenty-five to thirty bombers, climbing to assigned altitudes at the same time.[9] The hazard increased in the winter months. Eighth Air Force records reveal that approximately three hundred bombers and their crews were lost by collision during combat assembly—about 5 percent of all losses during the air war over Europe. Though the temperature would be below zero, pilots would sweat while jockeying their cumbersome aircraft into position during the nerve-wracking assembly procedure.

6. Each bomber had as many as twelve .50-caliber machine guns aimed in all directions.

7. From the German words for antiaircraft artillery—*Flieger Abwehr Kanonen.*

8. Later in the war the Eighth began dropping strips of metallic foil called "window" in an attempt to foul up the radar and aiming capability of the German 88-millimeter cannons.

9. The 384th was probably less affected by this geographical congestion than most other groups because Grafton Underwood was located at the northwest corner of the area accommodating the bases. Grafton Underwood had the distinction of being the launching point of the first and the last bombs dropped on the continent of Europe during World War II. The first was on the rail marshaling yards of Rouen, France, on August 17, 1942, by the 97th Group and the last on the Skoda Works at Pilsen, Czechoslovakia, on April 25, 1945, by the 384th. The pilot of the lead plane on the first bombing mission was Major Paul W. Tibbetts, who was later to fly the B-29 *Enola Gay*, which dropped the atomic bomb on Hiroshima.

The takeoff itself, an anxiety-producing operation even under normal conditions, was made more hazardous by the combination of short runways and heavy loads of bombs, gasoline, and ammunition. The B-17s and B-24s of the Eighth Air Force frequently carried weights well over their designed capacities.

In *One Last Look, a Sentimental Journey to the Eighth Air Force Heavy Bomber Bases of World War II in England*, a B-17 navigator told about a takeoff for a 2780 blues mission to Berlin :[10]

> The third plane to go gained enough speed to partially lift off the ground. Then it stalled and came down, and its gear collapsed and the plane went on down on its belly. Shortly after that there was a big explosion and it looked like that whole end of the field had blown up. The rest of us were then instructed to go to the short runway, where, with our full loads of gas and bombs, we had to make a crosswind takeoff.
>
> We really sweated that one out . . . but at the last minute the pilot bounced the wheels and got us into the air, and by then popping some flap he gave us an extra goose that just got us over the trees at the end of the runway.
>
> When we got back that evening we saw what the explosion had left . . . just a hole in the ground and two wings and a tail . . . but the crew had all managed to get out in time.

Like most of the bases in England, Grafton Underwood offered little personal comfort. The barracks lacked plumbing. The rather primitive latrine was located some distance away in a separate building, as were the washing facilities, which we called the Ablution Room. The showers were located even farther away in a communal site.

It was quite a chore to go out in the cold to take a shower. Consequently our cleanliness suffered, though the lack of facilities wasn't as bad as it had been at Bovington, where we were first stationed in England. Several of us at Bovington went AWOL for a few days, going to London, where we could take a shower or bath in a hotel where we stayed.

The prevailing style of architecture at Grafton Underwood, from the mess halls to the officer and NCO clubs was the Nissen

10. The number 2780 designated the maximum fuel capacity in gallons of the Flying Fortress.

hut. Barracks were dispersed, and some were as much as a mile distant from the flight line and other parts of the base, so we depended on bicycles for transportation.

The hut where I was quartered accommodated twenty men, four officers each of five different aircrews. The brass had better, less-crowded quarters. Heat was provided by a small coal-burning stove that stood in the center of the hut. Those closest to the stove were too warm, and those toward the front and the back of the barracks were too cold. Coal was rationed and carefully guarded. The sergeant orderly for our hut had a gift for obtaining more coal than the rationed amount, but when he was caught, he was demoted to private. He would regain his stripes, get caught again, and again become a private. For him this was a regular cycle. We told him he needed to get stripes with zippers.

*   *   *

Our crew spent the month of December 1943 and the first few days of 1944 in training flights, attending ground-school classes, listening to intelligence and security lectures, familiarizing ourselves with our new surroundings, and listening to our comrades-in-arms tell about missions they had flown. Some of the old-timers especially mentioned the mission to hit the ball-bearing factory at Schweinfurt, in which the United States lost sixty bombers. In mid-December one of the crews whose officers were quartered in our hut completed its twenty-fifth mission. The pilot showed us a chunk of flak shrapnel lodged beneath the plane's seat. A little higher and he might have been severely wounded or killed. "You've got to be lucky to make twenty-five," he said.

On January 5, 1944, we knew our introduction to combat was at hand. Neil Britt was assigned to fly a mission to Kiel as copilot for another crew, to gain experience before leading his own crew.

When he returned Britt told us how cold it had been flying at thirty thousand feet. "We had trouble getting the controls to respond," he said. "It must have been fifty below up there."

A young bombardier named Bean (we called him "Baby" because he was only nineteen) was also on his first mission that flight. Baby was awestruck by his first taste of aerial combat. "I saw a guy fall out of the bomb bay in the ship next to us," he said. We found out later that Technical Sergeant Fred Wagner had gone to release some bombs that had stuck, passed out from lack of oxygen, and fell out of the plane through the open bay. Months later it was determined he had revived in time to pull his parachute cord.

The Eighth Air Force lost twenty-five bombers that day.

★   ★   ★

The January 5 mission to Kiel was the 384th's last under the command of General Eaker, who was sent to Italy to take command of the Fifteenth Air Force. Commanding general of the Eighth Bomber Command and later head of the Eighth Air Force, Eaker had led the second squadron of six planes on the first mission from Grafton Underwood. The reporters gathered at Grafton Underwood to greet the returning Fortresses were quick to notice the name of Eaker's B-17—*Yankee Doodle*—and that's what his plane was called when the stories appeared next day. In a congratulatory message Sir Arthur Harris, commander in chief of the RAF Bomber Command, said: ". . .'Yankee Doodle' certainly went to town and can stick another well-deserved feather in his cap. . . ."

General Eaker was a thoughtful, articulate man who probably got along with the British allies better than any other American general. His writing skill has been credited with saving the U.S. armed forces practice of daylight precision bombing. British leaders, critical of this policy, wanted the Eighth Air Force to discontinue daytime missions and join the RAF in bombing Germany only at night. They argued that the losses would be less. At the Casablanca summit conference in January 1943, British Prime Minister Winston Churchill was intent on persuading President Roosevelt to switch to night bombing raids. When General Henry Arnold, commander of the U.S. Air Force, learned of this, he asked General Eaker to come to Casablanca to help present the case for daytime bombing to the prime minister. Eaker wrote a one-page memorandum, which he presented to Churchill, outlining arguments for continuing the policy. Churchill was intrigued by one particular sentence, ". . . if the RAF bombs by night and we bomb

by day, bombing around the clock, the Germans will get no rest . . ."
Churchill withdrew his effort to change the policy.[11]

★   ★   ★

Eaker was replaced as commander on January 6, 1944, by General
James H. "Jimmy" Doolittle, one of the most famous aviators in
America. A pioneer in instrument flying, Doolittle was a scholar as
well. He had attended MIT in the 1920s and received one of the
first Ph.D.s in aeronautical engineering. Doolittle had been
awarded the Congressional Medal of Honor for leading the carrier-
based B-25s on the bombing of Tokyo in 1942.

On January 7, I flew on the first mission under Doolittle's leadership of the Eighth, having been assigned as substitute bombardier
to another crew. The target was the I. G. Farben Industrie syn-
thetic fuel plant at Ludwigshaven.

I knew my time for combat was coming soon, but the message
from squadron headquarters that I had been assigned to fly with another crew the following morning came as a big shock. I slept fitfully that night, and it seemed I had just fallen asleep when I was
awakened by a flashlight beam. The bearer was a ground-crew
sergeant. "Time to get up, Lieutenant," he announced. "It's five
o'clock. Briefing's at six. Better get your gear together and then get
some breakfast."

What a feeling—like nothing I ever had felt before—a summons to battle. Until then I had only vicariously experienced such
an awakening through the cursing of the senior crewmen, their pro-
fanity, I thought, not as much due to being called to go hit the Nazis
as to being so rudely awakened at a God-forsaken hour. The nerve-
wracking nature of my summons was compounded by the realiza-
tion that my soon-to-be fellow travelers were relative strangers.

11. After another later meeting between the two heads of state, Eaker again displayed his skill with words. Roosevelt's plane, the *Sacred Cow*, had approached the
field at the same time as a badly damaged fighter plane, and the president's plane
was cut out of the landing pattern. Some of the aides in FDR's entourage complained. Requested to reprimand the young airman, Eaker wrote, "I must reprimand you for furthering the war effort by saving a valuable airplane and also your
own life. By so doing you cost the Commander-in-Chief an extra three minutes in
the air. Such acts as this cannot be tolerated."

We flew over almost complete cloud cover on the way to the target, and as we neared Ludwigshaven, I could see the Alps poking through the clouds in the distance. Because of the cloud cover, though, we had to rely on radar in the lead Pathfinder planes rather than conventional visual aiming.[12] We encountered quite a bit of enemy fire, mostly as we neared the target area. Soon after we dropped our bombs, we were attacked by four or five German fighters approaching the rear of our plane. Gunners yelled a warning to the crew, "Jerrys coming at six o'clock high." Seconds later, machine guns began firing. After a few bursts, I heard an exultant whoop on the intercom, "I got 'im, I got the bastard!" The tail gunner had shot down an ME-109. But a dozen of our bombers were lost that day.

*   *   *

Our crew's first mission together came four days later on Tuesday, January 11. Meteorologists had forecast clear weather for central Europe, affording the first opportunity in three months to strike at aircraft factories deep in Germany. A maximum effort by approximately 650 bombers was planned to attack five assembly plants in Brunswick, Halberstadt, and Oscherschleben.

Good weather may have been forecast for Germany, but England experienced its usual dreary conditions. Dawn began with murky skies. As soon as we left the coast of England, Britt ordered us to test fire our machine guns, a customary ritual. As the weapons fired, their recoil shifted the plane's course for a second or two.[13]

*   *   *

The B-17s had no heat, and the temperature at high altitudes was as much as sixty degrees below zero. To protect ourselves, we wore

12. Early in the war each bombardier used the Norden bombsight, aiming and dropping bombs on his own. Later, however, leaders of the Eighth learned that greater accuracy and more concentrated bomb patterns could be achieved by having experienced bombardiers in squadron and group lead planes perform the aiming and have less experienced bombardiers in other planes follow the lead ship's drop. 13. The authors of *One Last Look* noted ". . . A mere one-second burst from each of the guns in a medium-sized formation would throw out as much as three tons of lead to fall and sink to the bottom of the sea, and it has often been said that by the war's end the North Sea surely must have had a solid lead bottom. . . ."

layers and layers of clothing: long johns, flying suits, fleece-lined leather jackets, fleece-lined boots, and fleece-lined gauntlets over silk gloves. We couldn't touch metal bare-handed because our flesh would stick and become frostbitten. On a bomb run I would remove the gauntlets, but keep the silk gloves on to operate the switches and knobs to open the bomb bay doors and release the load of bombs. Some of the gunners, particularly those in the waist positions who were most exposed, also wore electrically heated flying suits, which they called "bunny suits." In addition, we wore flak jackets, "Mae Wests"(inflatable vests), parachute harnesses, steel GI helmets over leather flying helmets, oxygen masks, and strap-on throat microphones for communicating with crew members. We were so bundled up we could hardly move around in our cramped quarters.

The close-fitting oxygen masks became very irritating during the long hours we relied on oxygen. We also had to be alert to the dangers of moisture in the masks and oxygen tubing freezing.

★　★　★

That day marked one of the war's greatest air battles. The largest armada of aircraft the Eighth had yet dispatched struck plants that manufactured the Focke Wulf 190 and Junkers aircraft. More than 150 German fighter planes were destroyed and approximately sixty of our bombers were lost. I remember seeing a couple of bombers go down over Oscherschleben and firing a few machine gun bursts at enemy fighters, but they were out of range.

Most of the attacks came from rocket-firing ME-109s, and there was a report of German medium bombers trailing bombs from cables overhead. As we approached Oscherschleben I saw a huge explosion fewer than a hundred yards ahead of my position. The ball of fire and smoke was greater than a burst of flak, but not large enough to have been a plane.[14]

The mission marked the beginning of long-range fighter escort by the P-51 Mustang. Fighter escort before this date had been limited to the shorter range Spitfires, P-47 Thunderbolts, and P-38

14. There were rockets fired at us that day; the official Group report on the mission stated that ". . . staff sergeant Day of the ship piloted by Lieutenant Fioretti shot down one craft in a rocket firing formation . . ."

Lightnings. Although outnumbered four to one, the new Mustangs did a good job of defending their "big brothers" over Halberstadt, Brunswick and Oscherschleben. Mustang pilot James Howard shot down three enemy planes and was awarded the Congressional Medal of Honor for his valiant performance. Even after running out of ammunition Howard had made diving passes at German fighters to distract them from attacking our bombers. The presence of American fighters so deep into Germany surprised the Luftwaffe and made it wonder if the intended target that day was Berlin.[15]

For its part in the raid, the 384th provided twenty-two B-17s, and in view of the magnitude of the action, it emerged with relatively little damage. Eight of our bombers had been hit, but all returned safely, and we had shot down six enemy fighter planes.

After completing our mission we returned to England. As soon as we got out of range of enemy fire, I decided it was time to snack on a Milky Way candy bar I had brought along. But when I tried to bite into it, I knew I'd have to wait. It was frozen solid. About that time I noticed the top turret gunner in the plane adjacent to ours slip off his mask and put a cigar in his mouth. After a couple of minutes he would remove the stogie and slip his mask back on. I hoped he wouldn't try to light the cigar because we were all still on oxygen.

As we neared the French coast we encountered a sleet storm and we were forced to land at a B-24 base south of our station. After being debriefed and getting something to eat, we boarded GI trucks dispatched from Grafton Underwood to get back to base. The truck driver must have traveled the length of blacked-out Britain trying to find his way to the 384th. We finally arrived at Grafton Underwood—cold, stiff, and exhausted—in the wee hours of January 12, nearly twenty-four hours after mission takeoff. But for our effort that day, we were awarded the Presidential Distinguished Unit Citation.

15. Berlin had not yet been a target for the Eighth.

Operation Crossbow

★   ★   ★

We awakened early the morning of Friday, January 14. A sleet storm had cleared the skies, the sun was out, and we were looking forward to a visit to London. Neil Britt, Ray Haley, Ernie Lindell, and I were getting dressed to leave the base, and as he finished putting a shine on his fancy new brogans, Ernie remarked, "Got to look good, we may be going to 'Doo-la-glue' before long." With that, he exited our Nissen hut. "Gotta run," he called back. "See you guys later." Ernie apparently was thinking about the intelligence briefing we attended the day before, in which we were informed about the German methods of interrogation at the infamous Dulag Luft.[1]

Not long after Ernie left, a voice blared over the Tannoy: "Attention, all personnel. Stand by. All passes have been canceled. Repeat. All passes have been canceled. All air crew personnel please return to your barracks and await further instructions." Several minutes later, we were told to report immediately to the mess hall for lunch, then to report to group briefing at noon. Nothing like this had happened before. Our first thought was that General Eisenhower had decided to launch the continental invasion. Ernie joined us at the mess hall, having been turned back at the gate as he was about to leave the base. After a hurried lunch, we went to the

---

1. Abbreviation for *Durchgangslager der Luftwaffe*, which in German means transit camp of the air force.

briefing room, where we stared at the map, which covered most of the wall near the entrance.

As each crewman entered the room, he too stared at the map with disbelief. The red yarn marking the route of bomber formations into enemy territory stretched all the way to Berlin—Big B— the target we all fearfully awaited. For the past month and half the Royal Air Force had been hammering the German capital during night raids, and we figured the Fortresses and Liberators of the Eighth Air Force would soon be making a daylight strike. A mission to Berlin had been scheduled once before, but was scrubbed by bomber command shortly before takeoff.

The room became fogged with cigarette smoke as anxious airmen awaited the briefing, staring at the solid one-hundred-mile belt of flak guns girding Big B on the map. We couldn't figure why command would want to bomb Berlin this time of day; it would be dark by the time we reached the target, and the Eighth had never flown night missions.

We were speculating when Major William E. Dolan,[2] the group intelligence officer, strode in, smiled knowingly, and changed the yarn's path, stretching it over the English Channel to the Pas de Calais area. We breathed a collective sigh of relief. What a gag, I thought. But it wasn't just a gag; apparently someone thought it would relieve the tension wrought by the unusual events of the day.

Then Colonel Dale O. Smith, a six-foot, seven-inch-tall West Pointer who had taken over the 384th about the time we had arrived, marched up to the podium and began to explain that "this was a hurried affair" (we already knew that)—a sudden bomber command decision to strike at launching sites of German rockets aimed at Britain. The launching sites had been mushrooming along the coast from Belgium to Le Havre faster than the RAF and Eighth Air Force bombers and fighters could knock them out.

The first mission in the Eighth's campaign to destroy the sites, called Operation Crossbow, had been flown three weeks before, on Christmas Eve 1943. From then until the end of August, 1944, more than sixteen thousand sorties were dispatched at a cost of more than

2. William "Pop" Dolan, the only staff officer to have served at Grafton Underwood during the 384th's 316 missions, was, without a doubt, its most beloved member, as well as its oldest. He was a "retread," having been a pilot in World War I with the famous Lafayette Escadrille.

sixty bombers. Despite regular obliteration, construction of new sites outpaced the rate of destruction. However, it was not until after D-Day that the Germans were able to begin blasting London with the V-1 robot (the British dubbed them "doodle bugs") and the V-2 rocket bombs. The siege against London and surrounding area claimed about thirty thousand lives that summer and finally ended September 1, when Allied ground troops overran the launching areas.

Our target was about twenty miles inland, near the village of Le Meillard, not far from Abbeville. Intelligence photos showed the target, but it was so well camouflaged it looked like just another patch of woods. Takeoff was scheduled for one o'clock, which gave us barely fifteen minutes to gather our paraphernalia, find a truck, go out to the plane, load the guns, check the bomb bay, start engines, and taxi to the runway.

We all pitched in to help the ball turret gunner, Bill Argenbright, set his guns in place. The rest of them could be tended to in the air. I ran up to the bomb bay and surveyed the load—twelve five-hundred-pound demolition bombs. Everything seemed to be in order, so I crawled into the nose of the Fortress, installed my guns and loaded them. In a matter of seconds we were rolling to the runway for takeoff.

We were speeding down the blacktop when Ernie began searching for his parachute. He was still upset about missing his leave, and this certainly added to his distress. I told him to call Britt on the intercom, but he threw a handful of maps, saying, "The hell with it. I won't need the darn thing anyway." By the time I found his parachute in the passageway between the pilots' seats, we were in squadron formation, approaching the English coast. Ernie handed me a map and asked me to give him a hand. The crazy-quilt pattern of the English landscape soon gave way to the smooth blue of the English Channel twelve thousand feet below. I called Clarence Wolfe, the tail gunner, and told him to look at the White Cliffs of Dover growing smaller and smaller as we moved toward France. I couldn't know it would be nearly a year and half before we would see that shoreline again. I checked my map and identified the mouth of the Somme River, our checkpoint, and thought about what a "milk run" this was going to be. In a few more minutes we would drop our bombs, then head home and take that delayed visit to London.

Suddenly we realized this would be no "milk run," no matter

how short the distance into enemy territory. Big bursts of flak began popping all around the Fortresses a mile or so ahead of us. Seconds later we were in the midst of it—wading warily through black and orange colored smoke puffs from bursting 88-millimeter antiaircraft shells. The antiaircraft fire followed us relentlessly and accurately. Then, about a half mile ahead, a Fortress was hit and began a vertical climb, its elevator controls shot away. It suddenly stalled and began falling in a flat spin, dropping like an autumn leaf. White billows of silk began forming in its wake. Any thought that this was a snap raid was forgotten.

We were on the bomb run now, and evasive action was out of the question. Besides, it would have been futile at the altitude we were flying, about fifteen thousand feet lower than normal.[3]

Flak was bursting closer and I could hear it. Not loud. Just a dull thump, thump, thump, then a whistle from the hot fragments of bursting shells whipping through the sky. I felt a tap on my shoulder and looked around at Ernie. Blood was oozing from his left arm, soaking through layers of flying gear. We were near the aiming point of the run, so I signaled I would help him as soon as the bombs were away. I opened the bomb bay doors, flipped all rack switches, hunched myself to get as much protection as possible from my steel helmet and flak vest, and watched for the drop signal from Lieutenant Jim Brown, the lead ship's bombardier.

We passed over the target without unleashing our load, then made a 180-degree turn for another run at the site. At our elevation the German gunners had a dead bead on us. I held my breath, waiting to be blown out of the sky at any moment.

Suddenly the plane shuddered violently, and I knew we had been hit. The number four engine stopped, and the propeller began windmilling and vibrating. The hydraulic lines had been shot away, and Haley couldn't feather it.[4] The ship began to shake; I could see the hub of the propeller turning jerkily and out of balance. The engine was falling to pieces like peanut brittle. Piston rods, cowling, nuts, bolts, and other assorted bits dropped out.

We were lagging far behind the squadron and losing altitude.

3. The usual elevation was twenty-seven thousand to twenty-nine thousand feet.
4. *Feathering* meant to turn the propeller blades parallel to the air flow, thus making them stop turning with the wind, or *windmilling*.

Our position in the formation had been number two, abreast of the lead ship, but now we watched helplessly as ship after ship passed by. I saw the formation drop the five-hundred-pounders, then wait a few seconds, trying to judge when we would reach the release point. We salvoed our load, and I traced the descending bombs by eye until they burst into a huge billow of black smoke in the clump of trees below. If the launching sites were hidden there, they were hit.

Meanwhile, the damaged engine, the right outboard, was shaking loose from the wing. Sheets of flame trailed from what was left of it. I was afraid the plane would explode momentarily. "Prepare to bail out, prepare to bail out," Britt yelled over the interphone. I looked around at Ernie as if to ask if he heard what I had. The expression on his face was answer enough. We ripped off our Mae Wests and flak vests, picked up our parachutes, and buckled them to our harnesses.

As soon as the parachutes were buckled, Britt gave the order to bail out. I motioned to Ernie to go to the escape hatch. He seemed reluctant and gestured to me to go first. I crawled out to the corridor between the pilot's and copilot's seats. When I stood up there, I saw Britt and Haley adjusting the automatic flight control knobs, trying to keep the plane level as possible for our bailout. But the plane continued its convulsive behavior, and I decided to wait no longer. I knelt near the hatch and pulled the red emergency handle. The door was swept into the slipstream. I hesitated a few seconds, then summoned enough courage to roll into space. It felt strange—not like falling at all. I seemed to be floating—until I pulled the rip cord and felt a terrific jolt. Every bone in my body seemed to snap, and I blacked out momentarily. I awoke to see a reassuring white mushroom above me—a brand-new RAF parachute the equipment sergeant had given me the day before. I looked around and saw nine other chutes, spaced a few hundred yards apart, and began wondering what I'd do when I reached the ground. In contrast to the ear-splitting vibration of a dying four-engine bomber, it was eerily quiet. I felt suspended in a void. The sky was bright and cloudless—except for the puffs of flak from the antiaircraft guns below—and no wind stirred.

Though the air was still during that brief descent to French soil, my thoughts tumbled endlessly. What in heaven's name am I doing here, I thought. What will happen to me? Will my folks hear of this? Will I ever see them or my home again? Then I began thinking about what we had been instructed to do if we were shot down. We had been told to head south and travel at night, resting and hiding during the day. We were given escape kits containing French and German money, a small compass, and fake identification cards with a photograph showing us dressed in clothing a typical young Frenchman would wear. I had worn a dark blue beret for my photograph. We had been told we should try to secure help, but to be careful in doing so, and to try to reach Spain, a neutral country some distance away, rather than to attempt the shorter route north.

Below I saw running figures and supposed they were French children. A couple hundred yards closer, I saw the "French children" were carrying rifles. The enemy would greet me before I had a chance; the escape instructions would not be put to use. I could see the guns aimed skyward and heard rifle fire. My God, I thought, those bastards are shooting at me! I hoped the shots were just a warning. The feeling of being suspended mid-air stopped. The ground seemed to be rushing toward me fast, and I was headed directly for a tree. I maneuvered the shroud lines of my parachute, barely missing the branches, and fell into a muddy bomb crater near the base of the tree. Just as I unbuckled the parachute harness, two young German soldiers appeared at the crater's edge, yelling excitedly. I was facing two Mauser rifle muzzles, so I raised my hands and climbed out.

The soldiers searched me hurriedly, seemingly disappointed at not finding me armed, then led me to a nearby flak battery, probably the one that had shot us down. A Luftwaffe officer in charge questioned me in fairly good English, addressing me as "Lef-tenant," until his interrogation was interrupted by bomb blasts from a formation of Fortresses overhead. A grinning, gold-toothed German noncom pushed me into a foxhole with him, jabbering in a mixture of languages. All I could make out was "For you der var is offa."

Hardly. I was on the receiving end of the 384th's raid. Five-hundred-pound explosives were thundering all around, shaking the ground and making my teeth chatter. The blasts even drowned the steady bursts of nearby 88-millimeter cannons firing at the bombers.

After the bombing raid ended the Germans confiscated my boots, helmet, and flight suit and marched me to an ancient, broken-down truck parked about a quarter of a mile from the battery. It was now about four in the afternoon and turning dark and cold. I wore only khaki pants and a shirt, not nearly enough for comfort.

On the way to the truck I saw a German soldier with a young girl, about seventeen or eighteen years old. She smiled at me and asked, "l'Anglais, Monsieur?" In my best schoolboy French I replied, "Non. Je suis Americain."

Neil Britt and Don Tucker, the last two to bail out of the ship, were already in the truck, surrounded by German soldiers puffing away on Britt's cigarettes. Britt whispered that he had seen Ernie Lindell near a haystack not far away. Britt and Tucker had distracted the Germans, allowing Ernie to hide.

Our plane had crashed not far from the truck. We saw smoke and flames coming from a wooded area and heard the machine gun cartridges from the fiercely burning B-17 exploding all around us. We tried to make the Germans realize we might be hit by the exploding ammunition and tried to convince them to drive the truck out of the vicinity. They were, to our dismay, unconvinced.

Finally they started the truck and drove us through the town of Abbeville to a farmhouse a couple of miles out of town, the apparent headquarters of the Luftwaffe forces in that area. In the main room, a painting of Hermann Goering was prominently displayed. This probably was the home of the notorious Goering "Yellow-Nosed" Messerschmitt fighter squadron, the aces of the Luftwaffe known as the Abbeville Kids.

We were searched thoroughly then and taken to an air-raid shelter, a small damp room in which there were several crude straw beds. A short while later supper was delivered—sour cabbage stew, a few slices of black bread, and ersatz coffee that wasn't even luke-warm. As we were eating, three or four men, apparently crew from the plane we had seen shot down by the first barrage of flak, came into the room. We were wary they might have been German plants, who would try to get us to reveal information. I could tell they harbored the same suspicion. This mutual wariness limited conversation drastically until both groups concluded neither was a plant.

Later that night Bill Argenbright, Morton Harris, Conway

Nichols, and Mort Mason from our crew arrived. Mason laughed about his hesitation in bailing out of our burning plane. "Man, piston rods, nuts, bolts—every kind of junk was flying through the air. I was afraid of getting hit if I jumped," he said. Only Ernie Lindell, Ray Haley, and Clarence Wolfe were missing. Wolfe was brought in the next morning, and Haley showed up several hours later. He had hidden in a ditch all night amidst a RAF raid. The next morning, he had sought help from some farmers, who turned him over to the Germans.

Sunday morning, January 16, we were loaded into a truck bound for Paris, a journey of less than a hundred miles, which took all day. On the outskirts of Rouen, the charcoal-burning jalopy had a couple of flat tires that kept us stranded in the cold for several hours. When the truck puffed into Paris about six that night, we were hungry, depressed, and miserably cold. In the City of Light we were transferred to a bus, where two tired guards faced us, cradling machine guns in their laps. I toyed with the notion of trying to disarm them, but soon dismissed it. On the way to the rail station we saw several boys, eleven or twelve years old, puffing cigarettes. Civilians eyed our bus with mild curiosity; thankfully, we were in France.

German civilians, I found out later, in many instances had set upon POWs with pitchforks, sticks, whatever kind of weapon was at hand. In some instances American and British fliers arriving in Germany were executed by enraged civilians. To the Germans, their homes destroyed, family members wounded or killed in the air war, we were "Luft Gangsters," or "Terror Fliers." We were safer with the German soldiers, disciplined in the rules of war set forth in the 1929 Geneva Convention accord, than with civilians.

Our captors wasted no time getting us onto a train headed for Frankfurt Au Main, from where we were to be taken to Dulag Luft for interrogation. The guards on the train couldn't speak English, and we didn't know German, so we couldn't make them understand we were famished. We hadn't eaten in more than twenty-four hours and nothing good since before the mission Friday. About an hour after leaving Paris we finally were given some sausage and a few chunks of foul-tasting black bread. To us at the time it was as good as a meal in a four-star restaurant.

We stopped in Rheims for a few minutes to change trains. The station was jammed with green-clad Wermacht troops and military supplies.

I slept fitfully in the crowded compartment that night, awakened frequently by memories of the past three days and thoughts of my uncertain future. But most of my thoughts and dreams were about food; hunger can drive all other thoughts out of mind.

Interrogation
at Dulag Luft

★ ★ ★

e rolled into the Frankfurt station early Monday morning, January 17. We stood in the bitter cold for several minutes, objects of hostile stares from embittered German civilians, then boarded a trolley for Dulag Luft, located outside the town of Wetzlar, a few miles north of Frankfurt.

As we approached the large, drab building known to prisoners as "the hotel," I saw a group of shabby, once-proud fliers being marched to another trolley that would start them on their way to a permanent prisoner of war camp. One prisoner's right arm was in a sling. He had other injuries, too, and walked with great difficulty.[1]

As soon as we arrived at Dulag Luft, we were again searched. This time we were ordered to strip completely; our clothing was examined painstakingly. The guards kept my class ring, watch, rosary, and dog tags, but returned my clothes. After dressing I was taken to a six-by-nine bare cell with a small frosted glass window,

1. Later, I learned he was a B-26 pilot who had gone down on a mission to Holland. His plane had exploded, and the next thing he remembered was tumbling through the air still strapped to his armor-plated seat. He managed to pull the ripcord on his parachute and unbuckle from the seat. Shedding the weight slowed his descent, but he landed in a tree. A few hours after he fell he was treated by a German doctor, who told him his right arm, shoulder blade, and collarbone had been broken. Six other crewmen in his plane were killed in the explosion.

37

located several feet from the floor and barred from the outside. Beneath the window was an electric radiator and against one wall was a table and chair. Opposite was a narrow bunk with a straw mattress, a threadbare blanket, and a thin straw pillow.

Solitary confinement. I had been briefed, but no amount of briefing could have adequately prepared me for this experience. The interrogation methods at Dulag Luft were based upon the premise that if a prisoner was deprived of contact with others, put on a starvation diet, and subjected to other discomforts, he would soon be willing to talk, or to unwittingly reveal information that would help the Nazi war effort. There was nothing to do but sit, lie down, sleep, count the nails in the ceiling boards, pace the floor, think, and wonder what might lie ahead. Prison camp seemed welcome at this juncture—anything to get away from being alone and hungry in a cramped, cold, dreary cell. Food was almost nonexistent. For breakfast I had a slice of that infamous black bread of mysterious ingredients, followed at noon by a cup of sauerkraut soup, and at supper another slice of bread.

A sign on one of the walls warned of punishment for writing on the walls or otherwise defacing any part of the cell. Big deal. Were we going to be executed for marring the decor? In defiance of the Nazis, my cell walls were scratched with Vs for Victory, names of former inmates, and the inevitable "Kilroy was here." I tried to communicate with the prisoner next door by tapping Morse code messages on the wall, but I got only feeble, indecipherable responses and gave up. Solitude and starvation were getting to me. I began to wonder when I would be subjected to interrogation and, in fact, found myself looking forward to it as a relief from the monotony of my imprisonment.

Interrogation began my second day, though I didn't realize it at the time. A man in civilian dress, who identified himself as a Red Cross representative, entered my cell that night and asked me to fill out a lengthy form, which he said was necessary before being sent to a prison camp. He told me I would have to establish my identity before leaving Dulag Luft. "This is for the Red Cross," he said with a smile. I studied the form. The first three lines appeared to be legitimate inquiries, but the farther down I read, the more suspicious I became. I wondered if he thought I was stupid enough to believe the Red Cross wanted to know what bomb group I was from, who my commanding officer was, or what our bomb load had been. I filled in my name, rank, and serial number—the only information prisoners of war were required to provide according to the Geneva Convention—and handed the form back to him. His politeness vanished. Angrily he told me that my "uncooperativeness" might delay my release from solitary confinement or even result in my being turned over to the Gestapo as a spy. He left and I went back to counting nails.

Two days later a guard came and took me to another building. He led me into a large office, in the far corner of which a middle-aged, balding Luftwaffe officer sat behind a large desk. He beckoned me over and asked how I had spent the night.

"Too cold," I said.

"A little cooperation on your part might shorten your stay here," he replied. Then he asked how many cigarettes I smoked a day. I wondered how he knew I was a smoker and without thinking I told him I smoked about a pack a day. He offered me a cigarette from a pack labeled West Point. Tobacco was scarce in Germany; I wondered where he had obtained it, but I accepted the cigarette nonetheless. I hadn't smoked in a week, and the first drag set the room spinning.

I half-expected my interrogator to aim a glaring spotlight on me and start grilling. Instead, he aimed facts.

"You are from the 547th squadron of the 384th Bomb Group located at Grafton Underwood, England. Your squadron commander is Captain Horace Frink, and the CO of the 384th is Colonel Dale O. Smith. Here is your squadron insignia," he said, pointing to a familiar round leather patch we wore on our flight jackets when not flying over enemy territory.

I was flabbergasted. I learned more about my group and the tactics of our bomber formations from this German than I had from our own military. He opened a large photo album and showed me photographs of some former members of the 384th who had been "guests" at the "hotel."

After the war, German intelligence officers revealed how some bits of information helped them identify a prisoner's group. In our escape kits were fake IDs, with photographs of us clad in civilian garb. Mine, for example, showed me wearing a dark beret and nondescript clothing similar to what a Frenchman in his early twenties might wear. The same clothing might be worn by another flier for an ID photograph. By comparing photographs with previously identified prisoners, the Germans might then discover the group affiliation of a captured airman. Another clue might be on a man's PX card. A group's PX counter might have had a distinctive woodgrain, which left markings on the card. PX cards were compared to others acquired and identified earlier.

The interrogator impressed me with the magnitude of information he had about me and my military organization. Our intelligence officers warned us that the German interrogators would use this tactic, still it startled me—which was the whole idea. German intelligence wanted Allied prisoners to believe intelligence knew so much about the prisoners and their outfits that talking wouldn't hurt and would help the prisoners get out of the miserable place. But, of course, German intelligence *didn't* know all it wanted to know, or it wouldn't have gone to such lengths to find out more.

The Hauptmann seemed to have been thinking, as I did before the Friday briefing, that our raid might be a prelude to a coastal invasion of France. Any information about the raid might be valuable to the Nazi strategists, who no doubt had invasion jitters. Actually the raid was no prelude, but rather a strike on the launching sites of the buzz bombs that were to pound London and surrounding parts of England about six months later, but I was careful not to reveal this information.

After smoking another West Point, I was returned to my room in the "hotel." As the lonely hours dragged on, my impatience magnified. During sweeping time the following morning, I hailed a medical officer passing through the hall and asked him if he knew how long I might have to stay at Dulag Luft. He no doubt immediately notified the interrogation officer, because I was again called in for questioning.

The officer knew I was tired of the monotony of solitary, and he threatened me with punishment at the hands of the Gestapo if my refusal to identify myself continued. I told him I had already done so by giving my name, rank, and serial number. However his idea of identifying myself was to tell him what our target had been and what our bomb load had been. I didn't get any cigarettes that visit.

On the sixth day I was brought before the questioner for the third time. Now he seemed anxious. I got the impression that new POWs were headed for Dulag Luft and that the Germans wanted to move my group out to make room. After relating a disturbingly accurate chronology of my training program, the officer told me most of my crew had already left for prison camp and, if I answered one question, I could leave the following morning. He still wanted to know my bomb load, which might have provided a clue to our target. I thought about lying or satisfying him with a compromised response. But what if he was laying a trap? It occurred to me that he already knew the target, or could soon find out. When I was captured, I had in my pocket twelve cotter pins I had removed from the tails of the bombs to arm them when we were aloft. Ordnance expected the pins to be returned after a mission was completed. Attached to each pin was a tag, on which was printed the type and weight of the bomb, in this case, five hundred pounds. What the hell, I thought, I'm too tired to parry any longer. Besides I suspected the NCOs who captured me probably threw the pins away after the initial search. I decided to fib and hoped my questioner wouldn't find out about the fuse pins.

"We were carrying 250-pounders. I don't recall how many there were," I said.

I couldn't tell whether he believed me, but he said, "All right, Lieutenant, you may go."

I wondered if he meant I could go back to my cell or leave the "hotel." My unspoken question was answered that night when a sergeant came to my cell and returned my ring, rosary, and one of my dog tags. He gave me a receipt for my wrist watch, which he kept because he claimed it was U.S. government military property. Technically it wasn't, but I realized it would be futile to argue. He told me I would be leaving next morning to the transient camp in Frankfurt and from there to a prison camp.

In the morning, after the usual slice-of-bread breakfast, I was led down a long corridor, at the end of which a group of prisoners waited to check out. I saw Neil Britt and Don Tucker, my fellow captives at Abbeville. It was wonderful to see familiar faces again, even though they looked bedraggled. We discovered that the other crew members had already been discharged.

We were each issued a Red Cross capture kit—a brown cardboard box resembling a small piece of cheap luggage. It contained toilet articles, cigarettes, a sewing kit, chewing gum, and other such items. In addition we were issued a GI overcoat, sweater, shirts and pants, pajamas, GI shorts and underwear, and a khaki knitted cap, which was a helmet liner—the kind that "Radar" wore in the television series *MASH*. A German sergeant, who spoke very slangy American—he had been a stunt flier in New York before the war—told us about life in a prisoner of war camp and said we were to be sent to Stalag Luft I, near the town of Barth on the Baltic seacoast. Identification pictures and fingerprints were taken, then we were allowed to go into the barracks, where it seemed like old home week. I met several members of our provisional group from Oregon, nearly all victims of that January 11 mission.[2] We enjoyed the best dinner in nearly two weeks in the mess hall, which was run by French prisoners, and received some American and British cigarettes and a Red Cross food parcel.

Then we were marched to the nearby railroad station for a trip to our prison camp. We boarded two ancient cars, which were attached to the rear of any train headed north. There were about ninety POWs in my group, guarded by a sergeant and two privates. The latter couldn't understand or speak English, but the sergeant seemed to be fluent. One of the privates, aware that I had been a Fortress bombardier, tried to pick an argument with me about the Eighth Air Force bombing policies. But since we couldn't understand each other, it wasn't much of an argument. I gathered he was charging the United States with bombing churches. He made his point by touching the palms of his hands together, forming the shape of a steeple with his fingers, and vehemently declaring, "Dominus Vobiscum Kaput!" I showed him my rosary, shook my head in denial, and retorted, "Nein, nein." He wasn't convinced.

The week of an almost nonexistent diet followed by the sumptuous meal at Frankfurt threw my digestive system out of kilter, and I spent several uncomfortable hours on the second day of the journey.

On what I believe was the third night, we stopped in the rail marshaling yards of Berlin. The German capital had been hit by the Royal Air Force a few times prior to our stop, and we prayerfully hoped their bombers would lay off this target while we spent the

---

2. One of the prisoners, who had been assigned by the Germans to help out at the transient camp, was Lieutenant John Winant Jr., son of the U.S. ambassador to England who had succeeded Joseph Kennedy at the Court of Saint James.

night. We whiled away the anxious hours singing. After a few verses of "I've Been Working on the Railroad," "Off We Go into the Wild Blue Yonder," and others, the German sergeant asked us to sing our national anthem. I believe he wanted to embarrass us, thinking that many Americans didn't know the lyrics and had trouble hitting the notes. But we did sing it—with gusto. Many times I have heard a better rendition, but none with more heart and enthusiasm. And certainly not in a more unusual setting, or under such unusual circumstances.

I have often wondered what der Fuhrer would have thought about a rag-tag gang of "Luft Gangsters" singing the American national anthem in Berlin at the request of one of his Supermen.

Barth on the Baltic

★ ★ ★

We left the German capital early next morning, January 25, and passed through Anklam, then Stralsund. About three o'clock that afternoon, we pulled into the station at Barth, a small town in the province of Pomerania. A cordon of guards and a few vicious-looking shepherd dogs were on hand to take us to the prison camp, situated about two miles north of the ancient town.

Outside the barbed-wire enclosure of the camp, the group was officially greeted by a German officer, Hauptmann von Meuller, who appeared to have come straight from central casting in Hollywood. In fact, as he revealed, he had lived in Santa Barbara, California where he ran an antique shop before the war. He was all spit-and-polish, arrogantly polite, and charming, and he spoke perfect English with only a trace of an accent. The gist of his welcoming speech was that he hoped as much as we that our stay behind barbed wire would not be long. He boasted he would be back in the United States before we were.

Meuller was in charge of the intelligence department at Stalag Luft I. It was his job to quash escape attempts, almost all of which involved tunneling, and he did this rather well, considering the numerous tunnels his snoopers discovered during our incarceration. They located and monitored underground activity early on with seismograph equipment, but they would wait until a project was nearing completion before "discovering" it, then caving it in. While I was at Stalag Luft I no escape attempt was successful. On one of the nearly successful tunnel sites, though, Mueller posted a sign: Roses are Red / Violets are Blue / Tough Luck, Boys, We Found This One Too.[1]

After Meuller's introductory speech, we spent several hours in an empty barracks undergoing inspection and registration, which included the taking of photographs and issuance of the German equivalent of dog tags. The tags were made of two plates of a soft metal resembling pewter, joined by a perforation and stamped with a serial number and the words "Stalag Luft I" on both sides.

After registration we were permitted to shower, then assigned to housing. Neil Britt and Ray Haley were placed in barracks number seven, and I was assigned to number eight, in which most of the American occupants were men captured after the January 11th mission. Two rooms in my barracks were occupied by RAF prisoners shot down during the early days of the war. Several of these were from Northern Ireland. One was a British infantryman captured at Dunkirk.

* * *

Built in early 1940 to house captured Royal Air Force fliers, Stalag Luft I was situated on the shore of an inlet of the Baltic Sea, facing a small peninsula north of Barth. Stralsund was about thirty-five miles to the east and Rostock about the same distance to the west. The location may have been chosen for its remoteness, but more likely because the sandy soil and high water table were natural deterrents to digging escape tunnels. The most visible landmark was the spire of a thirteenth-century cathedral in Barth.

Originally both officers and noncommissioned airmen were imprisoned at the camp, each in separate compounds—an *offlag* for officers and a *stalag* for NCOs. The latter name persisted throughout the war, though it was a misnomer as the camp eventually housed officers only. In the spring of 1942, all POWs in Stalag Luft I were moved to other installations, but the camp reopened that fall when some two hundred RAF noncoms were transferred from

1. Nazi higher-ups thought Mueller's attitude toward American and British POWs too friendly, and a few months before the end of the war he was removed from his post and sentenced to three years in a Gestapo jail, along with a senior lager officer named von Beck, who was liked and respected by the camp's inmates.

Stalag Luft III, located about ninety miles southeast of Berlin. A year later, when the air war over Europe escalated with the entry of the U.S. Army Air Force, all of the British noncoms were moved to Stalag Luft VI in Poland, making Stalag Luft I an all-officer camp for British and American captured airmen.

When I arrived at Barth there were approximately eight hundred prisoners, about half of which were Americans, in the original west compound. About a month later U.S. newcomers were put in the newly established north compound. Two other compounds, north one and north two, were erected later as the POW population grew.

Each compound was enclosed by two barbed-wire fences, about ten feet apart and ten feet tall, with coils of barbed wire between them to deter attempts to crawl through. Guard towers, equipped with search lights and machine guns, were stationed at the corners and other strategic locations along the fence. A single strand of barbed wire about eighteen inches from the ground and twenty feet inside the fence encircled the perimeter of each compound. This was a warning wire no prisoner was allowed to cross, on order of being shot. Whenever a softball or football rolled into the forbidden area, anxious moments ensued. Prisoners had to gain the guards' attention and get permission to enter no-man's land. Trigger-happy guards were a constant concern. Several prisoners were fired upon, even some not near the warning wire.

Adjoining the west compound, in violation of the Geneva Convention, was a military installation—a facility for training anti-aircraft artillery gunners, which we called the Flak School. A couple of miles to the south was a small military airfield.

The west compound contained about a dozen barracks, along with a wash house/latrine and a building that served as a chapel and a theater. All were wooden structures. Barracks were about forty-five feet by one hundred or more feet and were elevated one to four feet from the ground on eight-inch round wooden posts to facilitate detection of tunnels and espionage by German noncoms we called ferrets.

S e v e n

The Spider Kelly Gang

★　★　★

In the camp barracks, twelve men occupied a room approximately fifteen by twenty feet. Double-deck bunks lined the perimeter of the room. Each bunk had a mattress and pillowcase stuffed with excelsior (fine wood shavings), a sheet, and a blanket. In the center of the room stood a wooden table, with a bench on each side. At one end of the room was a small stove for cooking and heat, fueled by briquettes of compressed sawdust and a petroleum derivative. Utensils consisted of a metallic pitcher and basin (which doubled as a cooking vessel and a pan for dish washing), ceramic bowls and mugs, and cutlery made of aluminum, stamped with the Nazi swastika.

★　★　★

First Lieutenant Sam Walker, a B-26 Marauder pilot from Brookhaven, Mississippi, who was shot down the day I was, served as our room commander. He and I had become acquainted on the train from Frankfurt and discovered that we had mutual friends back home. The ranking man of the twelve, sharp-tongued Sam was a raconteur who kept us entertained. He was an artful bluffer in barracks poker games, knew when to be conservative and when to resort to daring, and, as a result, invariably won, accumulating large supplies of cigarettes. He also was the best bridge player in the barracks.

Two room members, Henry "Mike" Mickelson and Zaven "Doc" Masoomian, had been in my training group in Oregon.

Mike was a potato farmer from Idaho; Doc was a radio technician with CBS in New York.

Mike was temperamentally suited to absorb a great amount of kidding. We tried often to get his goat and make him angry, but in all the months we were together, he never lost his temper.

Doc's moods were hard to predict. His outlook on the war fluctuated from hopeful optimism to woeful pessimism. He was happy. He was sad. Nothing between. When he was excited about something, he talked a blue streak. He kept us up many a night telling ghostly and fantastic tales. Doc enjoyed an argument, but frequently lost his temper—a signal he was being out-argued.

Bob Hosier, B-24 Liberator bombardier from Brooklyn, was also a first lieutenant. He had been on his second-to-last mission when fire forced him to jump. His face and right eye were burned, and he spent several days in a hospital in Rheims—a hospital, incidentally, built by the United States after World War I. Bob had spent nearly a month in solitary at Dulag Luft being grilled about radar, about which he knew nothing. But the Germans believed he did because he had flown anti-submarine patrols in the North Atlantic before joining the Eighth Air Force. Bob had the distinction of having more "shot-down time" than any other of our group. He was modest, conscientious, universally popular, and able to get along with anyone.

Four second lieutenants from the same Fortress crew were assigned to the room—Joe Tryens, Philadelphia, pilot; Norman "Pete" Burascano, Brooklyn, copilot; Earl Faris, Los Angeles, navigator; and Art Guinnip, upper New York state, bombardier.

Tall, lanky Joe Tryens was a quiet guy who spent most of his time carving intricate works of wood. I believe prison life bothered him more than it did the rest of us.

Pete Burascano had been a window dresser in Brooklyn. He was the best cook in the room, if not the entire barracks, and a wizard at manufacturing gadgets out of tin cans and wire. He even sculpted an excellent likeness of fellow Brooklynite Bob Hosier with clay from one of the many tunnels. With his never-ending energy and ingenuity for making things out of scraps, Pete helped make life in Stalag Luft I much more bearable. He may not have been expert in any one thing, but no one approached his versatility. His yen for French Elegante cigarettes, for which he traded precious Camels and Chesterfields, fouled the air, much to our discomfort, but besides cooking and carpentry, he provided the services of carpenter, tailor, tinsmith, mason, electrician, and barber. He also played a shrewd game of bridge and was foolishly reckless at poker. Whenever he wasn't tinkering, he read—he could finish a book in a couple of hours. But what amazed us most was the fact that this character was afraid that the war in the South Pacific might end before he could get out of Germany and join it.

Whereas Pete was a jack-of-all-trades, Earl Faris's expertise was more narrow. His forte was radio, which, having managed a broadcast station in Los Angles, he knew well. Also a prolific reader, Earl often perused two books at once. The camp had a small, limited library, and Earl was its most frequent patron. He didn't like fiction, as did most of us, but preferred technical literature. Besides his technical reading, Earl found time to study Spanish, French, German, shorthand, and calculus.

Art Guinnip, the youngest member of the room, celebrated two birthdays behind barbed wire and still was only twenty when we were liberated. One of the best softball pitchers in camp, Art had a fast delivery that helped our room defeat another in a grudge game on which we had wagered over two thousand cigarettes.

Dick Owens of Chicago was the funny man of the Spider Kelly gang, the name he coined for the residents of room three. Spider Kelly was the name of his favorite bar in the Windy City. An amateur cartoonist, Dick spent most of his time doing caricatures and sketching outlandish exaggerations of Allied airplanes.

Jim Pearson shared cooking duties with Pete Burascano for several months until we all finally agreed to take turns. Also a first-rate bridge player, Jim often teamed with Sam Walker in the barracks tournaments. When he wasn't preparing meals, Jim usually read adventure stories. But he was hot-tempered and always arguing with someone in the room.

Art Desmond, Boston's contribution to the Spider Kelly gang, took a lot of ribbing about his "hahvahd yahd" accent, but was quick on the comeback.

I was the twelfth member of room three, one of three rebels — Sam Walker and Jim Pearson were the other two—and one of four bombardiers, including Bob Hosier, Art Desmond, and Art Guinnip. I spent most of my time losing cigarettes in poker games and arguing with Sam Walker, my KP partner.

Before the gang was dispersed to other rooms, we acquired several new members. The first three were Francis Bornhorst from Indiana, Francis Villminot from Michigan, and John Aegeter from Ohio.

John Aegeter was from the 384th and had been a classmate at Victorville. He would perform others' KP for cigarettes, and he made model airplanes, wings, and insignia from solder, which he obtained by melting the seals on tin cans. He and Bornhorst moved to other rooms in the barracks.

John Kosky arrived in July. His B-24 had exploded, killing most of his crew. A veteran of twenty-seven missions, John was one of the top navigators in the Eighth Air Force and frequently flew with his group commander, Colonel Jimmy Stewart. In civilian life John had been a reporter for the *Los Angeles Times*, the *Milwaukee Sentinel*, and *Life*. We called him "Scoop." Scoop, who had written many articles for *Field and Stream*, talked constantly about hunting and fishing, his ardent hobbies when he had roamed the woods and lake country of his native Wisconsin.

Bill Hendrickson, a Fortress pilot from Yuma, Arizona, moved in with us in September. He had been shot down in April on one of the first American raids on Berlin. Like Dick Owens, Bill had spent some time before the war as a hobo, and he kept us awake a few times with stories of his wanderings.

Ben Spevack, a B-17 bombardier from Brooklyn and Chuck Lundsberg, a Fortress pilot from Michigan, were the last additions to the Spider Kelly Gang.

Ben, my KP partner for a while and one of my best friends, was energetic and happy-go-lucky. Once when I sprained my ankle in a touch football game, Ben performed all my chores and carried me around piggy-back. He was moved, with the rest of the Jewish men, to a barracks in the North compound in February 1945.[1]

1. Shortly before he was moved out, I asked Ben how he felt about being a Jewish POW. He replied, "When I was captured I expected the worst. So far, I've been a lot luckier and have been treated a lot better than I had hoped. I've been half-way expecting something like this for a long time and I figure it will get a lot worse. There's nothing anybody can do about it. I only regret leaving you guys."

Nothing happened to the Jewish POWs, but after liberation we found records and orders from the German high command that called for execution of all prisoners except Jews, who were to be sent to concentration camps. This order was direct from Hitler, but was wisely disregarded by the German military authorities.

Lundsberg didn't get along very well with anyone in the room and moved across the hall soon after coming to camp.

There were a few other kriegies at Barth I had known before.[2] "Duke" Hartsfield, a bombardier from the Fifteenth Air Force in Italy, was from Baton Rouge, Louisiana. I had known him before the war, and we spent many hours walking the barbed-wire perimeter reminiscing about folks we knew back home. He had been a frequent visitor to Saint Gabriel, and after the war he married a high school classmate of mine.

Another Baton Rougean was Royce Hatchett, whom I met on the train journey from Frankfurt to Barth. Royce had been wounded on his last mission and still had fragments of shrapnel throughout his body. So, of course, he became "Flak" Hatchett.[3]

I first met Jimmy Daigle of Lafayette, Louisiana, in the mess hall at Grafton Underwood. I met him again a few days after arriving at Barth. Jimmy had been shot down on his first mission, January 7, to Ludwigshafen. Before falling free from his plane Jimmy had slammed against the open bomb bay door, bashing his face, breaking several ribs, and getting knocked unconscious. As he swept past the ship's tail, the ball turret gunner, who had not yet bailed out, thought he was a German fighter plane. The gunner was about to fire when Daigle's chute opened, saving him from being blasted by machine gun fire.

A few weeks after I arrived at Stalag Luft I, a meningitis epidemic threatened the camp, but the efforts of the medical staff, a group of British Royal Army Medical Corps doctors who had been captured at Dunkirk, halted the spread of the dreaded disease after several cases had developed, one of which was fatal. It was at this time that Art Desmond was taken to the camp hospital with what eventually turned out to be appendicitis. At the time, however, we were afraid that he had come down with meningitis. We had noticed his disdain for the food we were provided, especially that foul black bread. We resorted to toasting it on the stove top to make it edible. It helped, but not enough to satisfy Art.

He was operated on by a highly regarded English surgeon from London's Harley Street, fashionable locale of many good doctors.

2. Kriegie was the Americanization of *kriegsgefangener*, the German word for prisoners of war.
3. Some forty years later I read in the Baton Rouge *Advocate* that Royce had received a much-belated Purple Heart.

Living Under Capture

★ ★ ★

O ur morning began at eight with roll-call formation on the parade grounds. During the winter we stood in the frigid wind anywhere from fifteen minutes to two hours or more while the Germans counted us. Roll call during summer was equally uncomfortable.

The men in each barracks, or block, formed into groups four lines deep. The German lager officer and several noncommissioned officers would then march into the compound. The lager officer exchanged salutes with the compound's top-ranked POW officer, then passed in front of each block, counting the men as he walked. As he completed each block he would give the count to a noncommissioned officer. Another noncommissioned officer walked along in the rear of each block, also counting. After their counts were tallied and compared we were dismissed until the next roll call at four-thirty in the afternoon.

On several occasions the roll call revealed that a POW was missing. In those instances a recount was ordered, sick-call absentees double-checked, and other authorized absences verified. If the recheck indicated an escape may have been made, we were subjected to a lengthy individual roll call. As each of our names were called we marched forward to a table, where a couple of sergeants checked our identity against the photograph taken upon our arrival in camp.

During one of these individual roll calls some of us decided to use the occasion to find out Doc Masoomian's middle name. He had steadfastly refused to tell us. When his last name was called one of us quickly yelled, "Which one?" The sergeant calling the roll appeared mystified, but he checked his roster and replied, "Zaven Nobar Masoomian." All the POWs guffawed and Doc stepped forward, glaring at us. The Germans couldn't figure out what was so funny.

After morning roll call our day was devoted to cooking meals, reading, playing cards, arguing, and sleeping. For exercise we walked laps around the compound perimeter and played touch football and softball. After evening roll call we were locked in the barracks until next morning. At the end of each barracks was a latrine for use at night. In the day we used a central latrine/wash house in a separate building several yards from the barracks. Lights were turned off at 11 P.M., but we usually had a bull session lasting until midnight or later. Time from lockup until lights out was usually spent reading or playing card games. Later, we organized quiz programs and debates.

The parade grounds also served as a sports field for touch football, softball, and, in the case of the west compound, baseball.[1]

Sports was a big time-killer during the long days, with softball games flourishing in every available space during the summer months. Each barracks sponsored a softball team and two leagues, the American and National, were formed. During the fall, six-man touch football was popular, and some rough and exciting games were played. In fact, the medical staff banned the game because the resulting injuries were overtaxing the small hospital's capacity.

In the south compound, where mostly RAF prisoners were housed, the favorite sport was soccer. Persuaded to try the sport, I was the only American on either of the teams playing a game one morning. They assigned me to the position of goalkeeper, because this position required the least skill in moving the ball.

*　　*　　*

Many of the camp guards were fairly young, but toward the end of the war, many of these young men were replaced by older members

1. Each compound had its own parade ground.

of the *Volksturm*, People's Army, so the younger men could help stem the diminishing supply of combat soldiers.

Some of the guards at Stalag Luft I could speak English, or enough English to get by in dealing with us kriegies. One who was proficient had been a steward on the oceanliner, *The Bremen*. A sergeant named Schultz had been a butcher in Brooklyn before the war, and that's what we called him, the butcher. One of the senior guards was reputed to have been a member of the Gestapo. During one of the numerous barracks searches he disturbed the sacrament in the room occupied by Father Charlton, a British chaplain captured at Dunkirk. The priest severely upbraided the guard.

Father Charlton, a red-headed Irishman of the Redemptorist order in London, taught classes in religion, which were popular with both Catholic and Protestant POWs. He conducted confession walking along the perimeter of the barbed-wire enclosure with the individual kriegie, as guards in the towers watched curiously. He frequently referred to himself as a "lion in the pulpit and a lamb in the confessional." Indeed he was. During our religion classes, he warned us not to regard our Russian allies as friends. "We just happen to be on the same side for now," he said. "But they probably will be our enemies in the future. They're no better than the Nazis."

Walter Amundsen from Wisconsin was designated interpreter for our barracks because of his fluency in German, and he dealt with the guards in our behalf. At night, when the German NCOs and their vicious dogs patrolled the compound, Amundsen frequently would go to the window of his room, knock, stealthily summon one of the guards, and offer a pack or two of cigarettes in exchange for forbidden items such as salt and pepper. The Germans loved American cigarettes and were fairly willing to barter with us. Walter even bribed one of the guards to obtain a Leica camera and a generous supply of film. Our barracks commander, Don Warren, had worked at the Eastman Kodak Company in his hometown of Rochester, New York, before the war. With the Leica, he took group pictures of the men in each room, as well as interior and exterior shots depicting the living conditions and layout of the compound.[2]

2. Some of the photos appearing in this book were processed by Warren at Eastman and sent to fellow POWs after the war.

★ ★ ★

Germany's treatment of prisoners of war varied, depending upon nationality, rank, and branch of service. POWs from Eastern Europe and Russia were treated worse than those from the west. Officers generally fared somewhat better than noncommissioned officers, and those who were in the air forces generally were better off than those of comparable rank in other branches of service. And all prisoners of war in Germany suffered more than Germans captured by the Allies, with the exception of those Germans captured by the Russians. The principal reason POWs from the United States, Great Britain, Canada, and Australia suffered less harsh conditions was that these nations, along with Germany, had signed the Geneva agreement concerning treatment of prisoners of war. Germany at least attempted to abide by the letter of the pact, because the Allied nations held far more POWs than did Germany. Additionally, the Luftwaffe controlled the camps housing captured airmen, and Hermann Goering, chief of the Luftwaffe, used his influence with Hitler to gain control of the prisons for fliers from the United States and Great Britain. Goering's chivalrous attitude toward his fellow fliers stemmed from experience as a German pilot in World War I.[3]

After the unsuccessful attempt to assassinate Hitler in July 1944, control of Stalag Luft I, and presumably all of its sister camps, was turned over to the Wehrmacht.[4] From then on, our treatment was more severe.

3. A manifestation of this attitude toward fellow airmen came to my attention when Lloyd Carville, a ball turret gunner in the 379th, told me about a recent reunion. A former pilot of the 379th, Charley Brown, had invited a former German fighter pilot to the reunion. During the war, Brown's B-17 was attacked by several Messerschmitt-109 fighter planes after a mission to Bremen, and he was nursing his badly damaged bomber back to England. As he neared the Channel coast an ME-109 closed in on the stricken B-17. The Luftwaffe pilot circled the bomber, and seeing the condition of the crippled plane with dead and wounded aboard, flew close, saluted Brown, and flew away. Brown noted the ID number of the German fighter and years later traced the identity of his adversary, Frans Stigler, the man he invited to the reunion. At the reunion Stigler told his former enemies, "I shot at planes, not helpless people." In September 1997, Brown and Stigler visited the Mighty Eighth Heritage Museum in Savannah, Georgia, where they taped a television program about their meeting in the European skies.

4. The Luftwaffe was the air force and the Wehrmacht was the army.

Throughout the war Heinrich Himmler tried to persuade Hitler to put him in control of all prison camps, arguing that only the Gestapo and SS could handle the obstreperous prisoners. In October 1944, Himmler's argument prevailed, bolstered by the Great Escape from Stalag Luft III by seventy-six airmen, principally British Royal Air Force officers, most of whom eventually were recaptured and executed.

Shortly after the Great Escape, camp officials warned us that escape attempts were to be more severely punished. Posters were placed all over the camp: "To all Prisoners of War! The escape from prison camps is no longer a sport!" The poster further warned of forbidden zones which, if entered, would result in the intruder's death.

Himmler's control of the camps was not total, however. Wehrmacht general Keitel remained in charge of the administrative duties of the camps, but with less authority. Due to the makeup of the Nazi bureaucracy and the decline in Germany's war effort, Himmler was forced to rely on established subordinates to carry out his policies, most of which were ignored or weakened by officers who feared reprisal after the inevitable defeat of the Nazis. Himmler's control, therefore, was limited in practice to POWs who had escaped and were no longer considered prisoners of war. Earlier in the war, a man who ended up in our barracks had evaded capture in Belgium for some time, but eventually was apprehended and turned over to the Gestapo, which considered him a spy and severely beat him. A while later, he managed to identify himself as an American airman and wound up in Stalag Luft I.

Although German military officers and NCOs were guilty of numerous crimes, it is clear that had prisoners been under complete control of Nazi police organizations, the prisoners would have suffered a great deal more. The SS and Gestapo had no regard for the provisions of the Geneva agreement. Quite a few Allied airmen captured by the SS and Gestapo were put into concentration camps. Some more fortunate were able to identify themselves as shot-down fliers and transfer to prisoner of war camps.

Germany did directly violate the Geneva agreement, however, by placing prison camps near military establishments. At Stalag Luft I, an antiaircraft training base and a military airfield were located just outside the fence of the south and west compounds. The camps making up the Dulag Luft complex in Frankfurt were situated close to military targets. Shortly after I left Dulag Luft in late January 1944, a bombing raid on military installations in Frankfurt severely damaged the transient camp there. Several POWs were wounded or killed.

The Germans were said to be proud of their honesty. And indeed they were honest in many things. They delivered Red Cross food parcels to us even when they had food shortages.

The Germans augmented the food packages with a few boiled potatoes of questionable quality, occasional carrots, and kohlrabi, a turnip-like vegetable. When we were in the south compound the Germans some mornings would provide a bucket of barley, which on occasion contained weevils.

Sometimes we would prepare cakes made of ingredients from the Red Cross parcels—ground GI crackers, powdered milk, sugar, and prunes or raisins. The batter would be poured into a pan crafted by Pete Burascano, our resident tinsmith, from flattened tin cans and taken to a communal bakery. It was heavy—we had neither yeast nor baking powder—but tasty. The Red Cross boxes also usually contained canned liver pâté, Spam, or corned beef. Occasionally we would be issued parcels from England, Canada, or other nations.

During our stay in the south compound we spent many a long night drinking tea with the RAF men. Once, we stayed up until about two in the morning frying potato chips, which we washed down with many mugs of tea. We used canned GI margarine to fry the chips. The only other use for this stuff was as material for candles.

I particularly enjoyed the company of five or six RAF fellows from Northern Ireland. My favorite among these was Paddy O'Malley, who was, as were many of the RAF contingent, shot down during the dark days of the Battle of Britain. One or two of the RAF fliers in our barracks were shot down in the so-called "phony war," in which hostilities began before war was officially declared. One of the men from Britain was an exuberant red-headed infantry private captured at Dunkirk. I don't know how he managed to be put into a camp for flying officers. But then I don't know how we also had a U.S. army ground soldier in our barracks. He was captured in the North African campaign.

Mail Call

★   ★   ★

Mail was probably the single most important thing in the life of us kriegies—surpassing even food. It reminded us, although our lives had in effect been put on hold, they eventually would return to normal. It also made us realize there were people who remembered and cared about us. Letters from home and from friends uplifted us from the depression and uncertainty of our isolation. Until we first heard from home we were uncertain that our loved ones knew we were alive. In my case it took more than four months to find out, and some took even longer.

We were limited in the amount of correspondence we could send, but not in the quantity we could receive. Each prisoner was allowed to write four cards and three letters a month. Cards were about three by five inches, and letters were five inches wide by about twenty inches long, with about twenty lines printed on the form. The letter form was folded three times and self-enclosed.

Wartime transportation problems no doubt delayed mail delivery, but the cards and letters we sent were further delayed by censorship—both by our self-imposed screening and by the German censors. We designated POWs in each block to examine all outgoing mail to ensure that it was not revealing anything of value to the Germans, and the Germans censored anything that cast them in an unfavorable light or appeared to be passing coded information.

None of the letters I received showed any evidence of censorship. Nor did I see any evidence of censorship in the stack of letters and cards I wrote that my mother saved for me. However, I did see a letter she received from the Office of Censorship in New York, dated March 30, 1944, which stated: "Your recent communication addressed to Lt. Oscar Richard, Dulag Luft, Germany, contained the statement that 'I do not like to have to type your letters,' which implies a possible writing restriction and may lead to misunderstanding."

"Letters to American prisoners of war in Germany may be handwritten and are not limited either as to length or number of messages sent. We call this to your attention and wish to advise that your communication to the addressee has been forwarded."

I am sure the thought of censorship inhibited us from writing anything more exciting than the letters parents receive from their kids away at summer camp. We were in a camp, of course, but a very different kind, and our messages mostly were assurances that we still existed.[1]

In reviewing my letters when I returned home, I noticed that practically all made some reference to mail, and usually it was the lead topic.

The first, a card from Dulag Luft dated January, 24, 1944, the day I was released from solitary confinement, read: "I am a prisoner of war in Germany—uninjured and being treated fine. Contact Red Cross for details and write soon. Crew okay. Notify friends and relatives. Permanent address later."

Five days later, after arriving at Barth, I dispatched another card to my folks: "Am now at a permanent prisoner of war camp in Germany . . . Get in touch with the Red Cross as to how to write and send packages. . . ."

A letter dated May 25, 1944, expressed my anxiety at not having heard from home. A couple weeks later, I received my first letter from home and immediately wrote back : ". . . You don't know

1. I learned after the war that my family got word of my capture from three different sources. The first was Ralph Haley, our copilot's twin brother. He was in the plane immediately to our right in the formation, saw our B-17 get hit, saw us bail out, and counted the parachutes. On his return from the mission, he sent letters to the families of our crew reassuring them we were alive. The second was the U.S. War Department, which first informed my folks I was missing in action, then a week or so later sent a telegram telling them I was a prisoner of war. The third was a series of postcards from shortwave radio operators around the United States who had heard Nazi broadcasts announcing lists of captured airmen.

how glad I was to hear from you, even though it evidently wasn't the first letter you have written since I was taken prisoner. Your letter was dated March 24 and postmarked March 30 from New York. Many of the boys who were shot down before me haven't received mail yet, so I feel lucky in having heard from you so soon. . . ." The subject of mail dominated my correspondence in the ensuing months.

Inevitably, of course, a few inmates at Stalag Luft I received Dear John letters. An RAF pilot received one from his wife in Liverpool, informing him she had been living with a private. ". . . But please do not cut off my allowance, though," she wrote. "He doesn't earn as much money as you . . ." Another kriegie was told by his wife: "I gave your golf clubs to a German colonel, a prisoner of war in a camp near here. I hope you don't mind." He wrote his wife, instructing her to get his "goddamn clubs" back and not to "give anything to the goddamn Germans." He heard later that his country club had canceled his membership "for not being a gentleman."

In several of my letters home I referred to cigarettes, mentioning in one ". . . receiving the 6 cartons of Camels you sent . . ." By arrangement with our families, several tobacco companies would send cartons directly to us in addition to the two or three packs included in the Red Cross packages. In another letter, I explained that cigarettes were ". . . our medium of exchange. For example a candy bar (American or English) is worth 50 cigarettes (65 for a Canadian bar). wrist watches [sic] have sold for anywhere from 1,500 to 2,500 cigarettes . . ."

Besides satisfying our craving, cigarettes were the basic currency of our primitive economy. During the early days of our incarceration, before mail and parcels began arriving, the value of cigarettes was high. When mail and packages arrived, inflation set in. The value of cigarettes for bribing the guards, however, remained fairly constant, as they didn't have any and really wanted them.

Cigarettes were used not only for trading for food and items of clothing, but also for wagering, especially in card games and lotteries, such as bets on when the war would end. Promissory notes (IOUs) and "checks" written on scarce bits of paper or cardboard from a Red Cross package were also used by habitual gamblers, and many of these were honored months and years later.

Ten

Colonel Spicer Sounds Off

★   ★   ★

Lighting in the barracks rooms was entirely provided by a single low-wattage bulb suspended from the center of the ceiling until one of our enterprising inmates decided to improve the system. Some fine wire, stolen from a tunnel-detecting device, was strung between the ceiling boards around the room and connected to slightly protruding nails in the ceiling above each bunk. Sockets, fashioned from Nescafé cans, were disconnected and hidden during the day. German soldiers traded light bulbs for cigarettes. Our contraband lighting system, however, came to an abrupt end one night near the end of 1944 when our security system uncharacteristically lapsed. A German sergeant entered our barracks room unannounced and stared, open-mouthed, at the lights strung around the room, whistled softly, then exclaimed, "Jeeeee-suuus Christ!" Thus ended our time of bright lights.

To warn barracks occupants that a German was approaching we stationed prisoners at the entrances to each end of the building. We took turns, each working shifts of three hours during the day. If a sentry spotted a German headed for a barracks, he would yell, "Goon Up," the signal to halt escape activity or to hide contraband. We told the Germans the word "Goon" was an acronym for "German Officer Or Noncom," but they later figured out this was an insult.

Occasionally an RAF bombing raid would provide a distraction. If it were dark, all lights in the camp would go out, and the kriegies would peer out the ventilating slots above the windows to watch the show. We saw the bombers of the Eighth Air Force go over for the first time on Easter Sunday morning, 1944. Rostock, thirty miles northwest of camp, was the apparent target, and we could see the smoke bombs, signaling bombs away, and feel the steady rumble of explosives shaking the earth. Father Charlton was conducting mass on the parade ground at the time.

Sightings of the armadas of the Eighth Air Force became more frequent as the war progressed and the bombers penetrated deeper into Reich territory. Each time the planes flew over, the inmates of the camp gathered outdoors to cheer their comrades. But most exciting were the strafing raids. RAF Mosquitoes would swoop down on nearby airfields and unwary locomotives so quickly the German air raid alarm system wouldn't go into action until the twin-engined fighters were winging their way back to England.

American P-51s hit a nearby airfield several times after escorting the heavy bombers on long missions. We saw one go down just off shore one afternoon, a trail of black smoke in its wake. The crews apparently were well briefed on the location of prison camps, because no matter how near to our camp was their target, we were not hit. We had our anxious moments, though.

After one particularly exciting strafing foray, camp authorities issued orders that no one was to be outside the barracks from the time the siren sounded the local alarm until the all-clear signal. It seems reasonable to suppose the Germans feared an attempted air rescue or weapon drop within the camp, because the order was strictly enforced and shots fired occasionally to discourage anyone who dared step out or lean out a window.[1]

★　★　★

We were moved to another barracks in the late spring of 1944 to make way for some RAF men, and in September our entire barrack was moved to a new compound for the same reason. The Germans were separating the Americans from the English and cre-

1. During one of the last raids on Berlin an American was outside cleaning a cooking pan, seemingly oblivious to the wailing siren. When his buddies warned him that the air raid siren had sounded, he attempted to climb through a window back to his room. He was fatally shot in the back of the head.

ating an ill feeling between them—which was the idea behind the plan.

The new compound was in command of Colonel H. R. Spicer of San Antonio, Texas, the ranking American officer. A tall, lean man who sported a distinctive handlebar mustache, Spicer hated all Germans and took no pains to hide the fact.

One morning after roll call, he rallied the entire compound to the front steps of his barracks and made an impromptu speech, for which he was court-martialed and sentenced to death for attempting to incite mutiny and for insulting the Third Reich.[2] I don't recall his exact words, but in part he said, "Lads, I want you all to remember one thing. Every damned German is your enemy, and I don't want any more friendliness between you and any of the guards and interpreters. We're still at war and, by God, if we have to sit and rot in this hellhole for ten more years we'll still be enemies with every German. Do you know what they did at Arnheim? They went through the hospitals where American and British prisoners were helplessly wounded and turned machine guns on them, killing them in cold blood."

He stopped speaking for a moment, turned to a couple of German officers standing a few hundred feet away and yelled, "And I'm not attempting to create a riot or anything like that, but you can go and tell your damned Kommandant what I said."

We were stunned by the Colonel's outburst, and we knew that tomorrow would find us under a new commanding officer.

A couple hours after the speech Spicer was arrested and marched to solitary confinement, where he stayed for several months. His death sentence was passed shortly after he was placed in solitary, but the order was never carried out.

No one envied Lieutenant Colonel Cy Wilson when he assumed Spicer's job. The Germans had been in a nasty mood since the attempted assassination of Hitler in July 1944. Control of all prison camps had been given to Himmler, the military salute gave way to "Heil Hitler," and camp regulations became even stricter.

2. Spicer was the third Allied commanding officer the Germans removed from command at Stalag Luft I. Soon after I arrived in camp Colonel William B. Hatcher, commanding officer of the 351st Group, was sent to Stalag Luft III for refusing to obey orders. And an RAF group commander was sentenced to a lengthy term in a Gestapo prison for inciting mutiny.

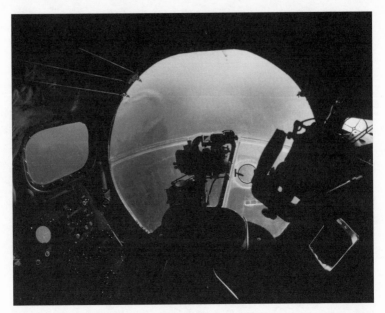

The bombardier had a front-row seat to aerial combat during World War II. In the center is the Norden bombsight, a closely guarded secret instrument that was capable of hitting the target with great accuracy. On the left is the instrument panel, which gave the bombardier the information needed to program the bombsight. To the right is a .50-caliber machine gun, manned by the bombardier before and after the bomb run.

Photograph by Dan Patterson, copyright 1994, *The Lady, Boeing B-17, Flying Fortress.*

B-17s assemble in combat formation amid the cloud cover over southern England. The letter "P" in the triangle on the tails of the planes identify them as belonging to the 384th. The "P" was chosen to honor the group's first commander, Colonel Budd J. Peaslee.

Photograph from the collection of G. K. "Dutch" Biel, 390th B.G. Published by permission of The Mighty Eighth Air Force Heritage Museum.

Oscar Richard's bomber crew posed in October 1943 for a photograph at
Grand Island, Nebraska, Army Air Base shortly before their flight to
England. Top, left to right: Clarence Wolfe, tail gunner; Morton Harris,
radio operator; Morton Mason, waist gunner; Donald Tucker, engineer;
Conway Nichols, waist gunner; (unidentified, replaced by Bill
Argenbright), ball turret gunner. Bottom, left to right: Neil Britt, pilot;
Oscar Richard, bombardier; Ray Hayley, copilot; Ernie Lindell, navigator.

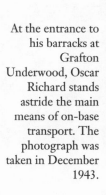

At the entrance to
his barracks at
Grafton
Underwood, Oscar
Richard stands
astride the main
means of on-base
transport. The
photograph was
taken in December
1943.

A view of the barracks and fencing at Stalag Luft I.
The Don Warren Collection.

POW Walter Amundsen, chief interpreter and "wheeler-dealer" of Oscar Richard's barracks at north compound 2, cooked meals on the small communal stove in the room.

The Don Warren Collection.

POWs at Stalag Luft I ate their meals at a table centrally located in their barracks room.

The Don Warren Collection.

Kriegies slept, chatted, and read in their barracks bunks at Stalag Luft I.
The two-tiered bunks, shown here, gave way to three tiers
as the camp's population increased.

The Don Warren Collection.

Kreigies staked their bets on cigarettes when
playing poker at the camp. Cigarettes also were useful
as an item of exchange with prison guards.

The Don Warren Collection.

Members of the Spider Kelly Gang at Stalag Luft I, with the dates they were shot down. Front, left to right: Ben Spevak, B-17 bombardier, 9/28/44; Sam Walker, B-26 pilot, 1/14/44; Francis Vilminot, B-17 bombardier, 9/11/44; Henry Mickelson, B-17 copilot, 1/11/44. Back: Pete Burascano, B-17 copilot, 1/11/44; John Kosky, B-24 navigator, 7/7/44; Art Desmond, B-17 bombardier, 1/14/44; Joe Tryens, B-17 pilot, 1/11/44

The Don Warren Collection.

More members of the Spider Kelly Gang. Front, left to right: Oscar Richard, B-17 bombardier, 1/14/44; "Doc" Masoomian, B-17 copilot, 1/11/44; Bill Hendrickson, B-17 pilot, 3/24/44; Art Guinnip, B-17 bombardier, 1/11/44. Back: Bob Hosier, B-24 bombardier, 12/30/43; Dick Owens, B-17 copilot, 1/11/44; Chuck Lundsberg, B-17 pilot, 9/28/44; Earl Faris, B-17 navigator, 1/11/44.

The Don Warren Collection.

Guards oversee POWs from a tower at Stalag Luft I
in December 1944.

The Don Warren Collection.

In May 1945, Germans fled the camp in advance of the
arrival of the Russian army. Kriegies dug trenches and foxholes
in case the army arrived firing.

The Don Warren Collection.

Due to recent food shortages, no POW was overweight when liberation came in May 1945. Pictured here are front, left to right: Bob Hosier, Oscar Richard, Art Desmond, Francis Vilminot, and back: Norman Pierce, "Commander" Harding, George Luke, Merril Hire, and Leonard Dahnke.

Ex-POWs board one of three hundred B-17s from the Eighth Air Force that landed mid- May 1945 in an airfield near the camp to evacuate some nine thousand former prisoners.

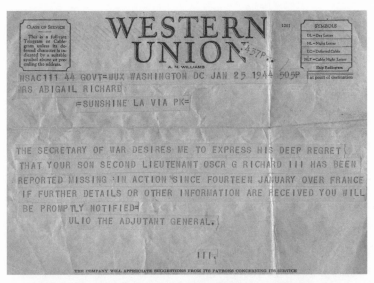

WESTERN
UNION

1201

A. N. WILLIAMS

NSAC111 44 GOVT=WUX WASHINGTON DC JAN 25 1944 505P

MRS ABIGAIL RICHARD

=SUNSHINE LA VIA PK=

THE SECRETARY OF WAR DESIRES ME TO EXPRESS HIS DEEP REGRET
THAT YOUR SON SECOND LIEUTENANT OSCR G RICHARD III HAS BEEN
REPORTED MISSING IN ACTION SINCE FOURTEEN JANUARY OVER FRANCE
IF FURTHER DETAILS OR OTHER INFORMATION ARE RECEIVED YOU WILL
BE PROMPTLY NOTIFIED=
        ULIO THE ADJUTANT GENERAL.

                III.

Mrs. Abigail Richard received this telegram on January 25, 1944, informing her that her son, Oscar Richard, was missing in action.

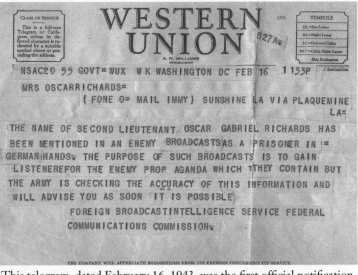

WESTERN
UNION

1201

A. N. WILLIAMS
PRESIDENT

NSAC20 55 GOVT=WUX W K WASHINGTON DC FEB 16 1133P

MRS OSCARRICHARDS=
        (FONE O= MAIL IMMY) SUNSHINE LA VIA PLAQUEMINE
                                                    LA=

THE NAME OF SECOND LIEUTENANT OSCAR GABRIEL RICHARDS HAS
BEEN MENTIONED IN AN ENEMY BROADCASTS AS A PRISONER IN =
GERMAN HANDS. THE PURPOSE OF SUCH BROADCASTS IS TO GAIN
LISTENEREFOR THE ENEMY PROP AGANDA WHICH THEY CONTAIN BUT
THE ARMY IS CHECKING THE ACCURACY OF THIS INFORMATION AND
WILL ADVISE YOU AS SOON IT IS POSSIBLE
        FOREIGN BROADCASTINTELLIGENCE SERVICE FEDERAL
        COMMUNICATIONS COMMISSION.

This telegram, dated February 16, 1943, was the first official notification
Oscar Richard's mother received from the U.S. government
about his POW status.

Kriegsgefangenenlager

Datum: JAN 24 1944

DEAR FOLKS: I AM A PRISONER OF WAR IN GERMANY - UNINJURED AND AM BEING TREATED FINE. CONTACT RED CROSS FOR DETAILS AND WRITE SOON. CREW OKAY. NOTIFY FRIENDS AND RELATIVES. PERMANENT ADDRESS LATER.

LOVE
OSCAR

Oscar Richard filled out this official postcard on January 24, 1944, ten days after his capture. The card is postmarked January 29, but he didn't receive mail back from his parents until nearly June that year.

Kriegsgefangenenlager

Datum: MAY 8, 1945

DEAR FOLKS: LIBERATED BY THE RUSSIANS A WEEK AGO TODAY, BUT STILL IN CAMP AWAITING EVACUATION. WE'RE ALL IMPATIENT TO GET BACK HOME AS SOON AS POSSIBLE. I'M FINE, HAVE PLENTY TO EAT AND EVERYTHING SO DON'T WORRY ABOUT ME. SEE YOU SOON.

Love, Oscar

Oscar Richard wrote this postcard May 8, 1945, but didn't arrive home until July.

Shown on the map are sites mentioned in the text pertaining to the
European theater of operations. East Anglia, an area ranging north from
London to the 384th's base and east to the North Sea coast was the site
of some 120 U.S. airbases, along with many RAF installations.

Map by Maradee Cryer.

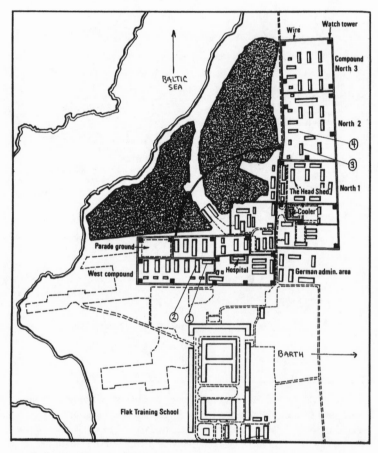

Stalag Luft I at Barth, Germany. North 2 and north 3 compounds
were added after Oscar Richard arrived in January, 1944. He was first
housed in the west compound in the barracks marked 1, then moved to 2.
Later, he was moved to north 2 compound, barracks 3. Colonels Spicer
and Wilson were in the barracks marked 4. Colonel Zemke was in
"the Head Shed" in north 1 compound.

78

Eleven

We Kept Informed

★ ★ ★

I n spite of our limited existence behind barbed wire we were better informed than were most Germans about events of the war. In some instances we learned of events before Americans back home did.

Stalag Luft I had a news service that put out a bulletin on D-Day several minutes before the New York newspapers issued extras revealing the invasion of the Normandy beaches. This kriegie chronicle, POW WOW[1] was founded and edited by Lowell Bennett, interned war correspondent for the International News Service. Bennett, who arrived at Stalag Luft I a couple weeks before I did, had wanted a firsthand view of the air war over Europe and was aboard an RAF bomber on a mission to Berlin when it was shot down.[2]

Men with radio experience assembled a small, but powerful radio from parts obtained through bribing German guards. The set, cleverly concealed in the wall of one of the barracks, was automatically tuned to the British Broadcasting Company network by touching two nails in the wall with a fine wire.[3] Each day, news reports were written in shorthand on pieces of toilet paper, which then were wadded in an empty wristwatch case and taken to another section of the compound to be transcribed and typed on

1. Prisoners of War Waiting on Winning.
2. Three other war correspondents were on the same mission: Edward R. Murrow of CBS and two Australian newsmen.
3. Probably the north 1 compound, where Bennett was housed.

paper no doubt obtained from a nicotine-addicted guard. The news sheet was typed with several thin carbon copies, which were secretly distributed to all fifty-some barracks each evening. The carbon paper was made by smoking sheets of paper over tin can lamps filled with GI margarine, producing carbon black, then sizing the sheets with smuggled kerosene.

The principal source of the news, of course, was the BBC news broadcasts, but other sources included accounts from newly arrived prisoners and even items from the German broadcasts. Bennett also received smuggled notes from couriers such as chaplains, doctors, and other POWs who were permitted to travel from one compound to another.

The Germans ultimately found out about POW WOW and made periodic attempts to put it out of operation, but were unsuccessful. They also suspected a radio was the chief source of news, but could never find it. One day, we were kept out of our barracks in the cold for at least nine hours while the Germans conducted a thorough search, to no avail. I never knew, and I'm sure that 99.9 percent of the kriegies never knew, where the radio was hidden. The Germans never found it.

When General Patton's tanks were racing like wildfire through France and Germany, news of their spectacularly rapid advance was distributed around camp by "security men." News received from BBC broadcasts was designated with a red star and was not to be discussed.

Maps were displayed in the halls and rooms in all barracks. Front lines were kept up to date with colored string markers pinned with phonograph needles. Lieutenant Melvin Brackendorff was our compound news officer and he did a magnificent job, despite his tendency to make the news seem brighter than it actually was. He made a bulletin board, which he installed in front of our barracks, and on it posted the latest developments that he translated from the Wehrmacht communique on German radio. He also posted a large map in our barracks hall and kept the front lines updated with a green pencil. Still, his accounts, derived from German sources, were consistently outdated compared to those received from the BBC news and issued to us via POW WOW.

Because we were often even better informed than our captors, we had to be careful not to reveal events not yet reported by the

German radio. We broke our silence, though, on June 6, 1944, when we cheered the news of the Normandy invasion. The German guards, not yet aware of the invasion, were mystified by our whooping and yelling. They didn't have a clue as to what caused our joyful celebration.

As might be expected the rumor mill also was active in our camp, and some of the rumors proved to be uncannily accurate. For example, I recall one of my kriegie friends, Joe Berger, telling me some details about a mass escape from our sister institution, Stalag III, more than two hundred miles away. What I heard then was strikingly similar to what I read many years later in a book written by an ex-POW, *The Great Escape*, on which the motion picture of the same name was based.

A man I met years later, John Welles from Ponchatoula, Louisiana, told me about how he forged the papers used by the escapees from Stalag Luft III. John was and is an expert calligrapher. John told me jokingly about trying to convince the German interrogator at Dulag Luft that he was an Episcopalian. John, whose middle initial is "E," was puzzled at the German's insistence in classifying him as a Jew. He then realized that the interrogator was looking at John's initials on his flight jacket.

Another rumor that made the rounds in our barracks had to do with experimentation with what was called "heavy water." None of us, of course, had yet heard about the development of the atomic bomb.

Twelve

Luminaries at Stalag Luft I

★　★　★

Several POWs who served time in Stalag Luft I were well known, gaining prominence before, during, or after the war. Among the U.S. Air Force luminaries was the ranking Allied officer and commander of the camp during the last few months, Colonel Hubert Zemke, head of a group of fighter pilots known as Zemke's Wolfpack. There were several aces in the group, including Zemke himself, who had twenty German fighter planes to his credit. Zemke went down October 30, 1944, when his P-51 Mustang, flying through a storm, iced up. The weight of the ice caused his plane to go into a flat spin, during which a wing came off, and his plane severed in two just behind the cockpit. He bailed out and landed near Hanover, where, after a day of searching for help, he was captured by civilians.

In *First of the Many*, John "Tex" McCrary had this to say about Zemke:

> I think Hub's outfit was the hottest in the Eighth while he was leading it. General Eaker (commander of the Eighth Air Force at that time) was sort of partial to him too. He told me about the first time he ever saw Hub:
>
> "I was at Wright field then. Mr. Henry Ford had decided that his production methods could turn out a lot of airplanes and he wanted to get one of our fighters down so his people could have a look at it. I arranged to send him a P-40. A second lieutenant reported in my office to make the delivery. He was a group

engineering officer at Langley. He walked in. Typical fighter pilot, chip on his shoulder, looked you right in the eye. Not insolent. Just confident. It was Zemke. . . . Colonel Hubert Zemke . . . is the ablest young man I have ever met. Far and away. . . . U.S. industry should comb the Air Forces after this war and grab guys like Hub Zemke."

In *My War*, Andy Rooney stated he had written several features about Zemke for the *Stars and Stripes*. One related an occasion when Zemke hit an ME-109 and the Luftwaffe pilot bailed out, his uniform on fire. Zemke saw the German writhing as the flames engulfed him. "I fixed him in my sight and fired to put him out of his misery," Zemke reported.

"No one who knew Zemke's sense of honor would doubt that he'd kill a man under those circumstances for any other reason than to save him from the agony of burning to death," Rooney wrote. "He was of the old school of gentlemen warriors. Eddie Rickenbacker and the Red Baron, von Richtofen."

Another member of Zemke's Fifty-sixth Fighter Group, Lieutenant Colonel Francis Gabreski, shot down thirty-three Nazi planes before becoming a prisoner of war. Like Zemke, "Gabby" was not shot down, but was captured when he crashed because the propeller of his P-47 plowed into the ground on a low-level strafing mission. Gabreski had been one of the few pilots who had managed to get into the air to fight the Japanese planes bombing Pearl Harbor.

Lieutenant Colonel Ross Greening, a flight leader on General Jimmy Doolittle's Tokyo raid and designer of the "twenty-cent bombsight" used on the mission, joined the fold at Stalag Luft I after his second parachute jump over enemy territory. After the war he organized a prisoner of war exhibit at Rockefeller Center in New York.

Another of the outstanding airmen was Colonel Henry R. Spicer, former commander of the 357th Fighter Group and senior officer in our compound, who was court-martialed. He and General Curtis LeMay[1] had introduced new formations and bombing procedures that improved the accuracy and concentration of bombing patterns and provided maximum fire power against

1. LeMay later became chief of staff of the U.S. Air Force and ran for vice-president with Barry Goldwater.

German fighter planes. Spicer had been shot down early in 1944, after his group had finished escorting several groups of bombers. A smoker, he took his group to a lower altitude where he could fire his pipe, and his plane was shot down by flak.

Second Lieutenant John "Red" Morgan was awarded the Congressional Medal of Honor for heroism on a mission flown July 28, 1943, a short time before his capture. His plane was hit near the German coast, and the pilot was mortally wounded by flak. Morgan, the copilot, took control, but the windshield was shattered and he couldn't see. Meanwhile, the engineer/top turret gunner had been shot in the arm. The crew's navigator bound the gunner's wound, buckled his parachute, and dropped the gunner out the nose hatch. He then helped Morgan remove the pilot, who was deliriously fighting for control of the ship, as well as for his life. Morgan moved to the pilot's seat, and for an hour and half flew the plane unaided. Morgan said he thought that Keith Koske, the navigator, was more deserving of the medal than he was, since Koske's quick action saved the life of Tyre Weaver, who received medical help as soon as he landed, and survived the war in a German prison camp.

Two missions later Morgan was shot down over Berlin, leading an attack on the capital. Unable to take evasive action on the bomb run, his plane was hit and exploded. Morgan was blown out of the B-17, parachute in one hand. He managed to buckle it to his chest harness and landed near a lake in Berlin.

A year later a newly arrived kriegie was in the north compound mess hall and hailed a man serving as a waiter, whom he did not know was a fellow prisoner. "Get me some sugar. This coffee is sour," he said. "I'm a combat airman." It was later pointed out to him that his "waiter" had earned the Congressional Medal of Honor and had been blasted out of a Fortress on a mission to Berlin, while the "combat airman" was an aviation cadet.

* * *

One of the biggest morale boosters in camp was the theater group, a collection of amateur and professional performers who staged several excellent plays, among them, *The Man Who Came to Dinner*, in which a young RAF pilot played a convincing female role. Two musical comedies were staged—*The Big Broadcast* and an original,

"Hit the Bottle," which was written and produced by Nelson Giddings, who later wrote the screenplays for *The Andromeda Strain* and *The Hindenburg*.

Both the north and south compounds had orchestras, manned by talented musicians, some of whom had performed with the big bands during their civilian days. The Southsiders, under the direction of Dorman "Shady" Lane of Al Donahue's orchestra featured "Buzz" Freshette, former trumpeter with Tommy Dorsey. The north compound Round the Benders featured musicians from the bands of Bunny Berrigan, Bob Chester, and Teddy Powell. The glee club in the south compound was under the direction of John Lashly, who had created arrangements for the Merrimacs, who performed for a national radio program in the United States.

★ ★ ★

One prisoner I had known during my days in the south compound became U.S. assistant secretary of defense after the war. I saw his picture in the New Orleans *Times-Picayune* in June 1979 and recognized him as Barry Shillito. I wrote asking if he wasn't the guy who played touch football with me in Stalag Luft I. He wrote back, ". . . I'm the same guy, but with different problems."

A number of other well-known personages who had been either captured airmen or who had flown with the Eighth Air Force included Nicholas Katzenbach, U.S. attorney general during the administration of President John F. Kennedy. Ex-B-17 fliers were Senator George McGovern, who was a candidate for the presidency; Lloyd Bentsen, former secretary of the treasury and vice-presidential candidate; and Tom Landry, former coach of the Dallas Cowboys.

Thirteen

The Final Winter

★ ★ ★

Stalag Luft I was located almost in the land of the midnight sun, about sixty miles from Sweden at 54 degrees north. During the summer months, the sun set about 11 P.M. and rose at 2 or 3 A.M. In winter, darkness set in about 4:30 P.M. and continued until 9 A.M. The Gulf Stream helped keep the mercury from dropping too low, but the ground was usually frozen solid for weeks at a time in December and January. Snow was abundant, and besides furnishing pretty scenery and recreational pleasure, it came in mighty handy once when the water supply was cut off for more than twenty-four hours. Buckets of snow were melted for drinking and cooking. And mixed with powdered milk and sugar, it made good ice cream. We found, though, that the best use of the great quantity of snow that fell during that severe winter of 1944–1945 was to pile it in drifts against the barracks to insulate them from the frigid winds that swept the compound. Even so, there were many nights we had to sleep with all our clothing on, including shoes and overcoats.

Thanks to the American and International Red Cross we had a better Christmas than we thought possible in a prison camp. We received special parcels containing canned turkey, plum pudding, jam, candy, nuts, dried figs, honey, and a pipe and tobacco. These were in addition to our regular parcels. The Germans showed the Christmas spirit by opening up all compounds until midnight and permitting a special variety show to be staged. Father Charlton held a midnight mass in the north compound.

To usher in the new year, we made a batch of wine from ingredients we had saved from our food rations. A shelf removed from the wall, nailed down to a bench, and waterproofed with tar made a pretty good vat, in which we dumped twenty pounds of raisins and prunes, six pounds of precious sugar, fifteen gallons of water, and a bit of yeast provided by one of the guards. Then we waited. The crude container began leaking and "Spider" Owens, self-appointed brewer, frantically went to work to keep the beverage from leaking out. Several other rooms in the barracks were in the brewery business also, and when New Year's Eve rolled around, sober members were in the minority. The brew looked like weak tea and tasted like formaldehyde. I think it had turned the corner from wine and was rapidly approaching vinegar by the time we imbibed.

★   ★   ★

The tremendous drive of the Russian Army in January 1945 raised havoc with living conditions in Stalag Luft I. German power lines were ripped away in several vital places, and our electric lights were out for over a month. The water went on and off periodically, and we were caught short several times because we had no containers in which to store water. Prison camps in Poland and East Prussia were being evacuated, and our camp was overtaxed with the men forced to move westward. Most were air force sergeants, and the rest were infantry men captured in the Battle of the Bulge. The latter were nearly all suffering from exposure and frostbite incurred during the long hike from the western to near the Russian front, then back westward to our camp in north-central Germany.

On the Spider Kelly gang's one-year anniversary together, January 25, 1945, it was forced to disband and move into other rooms in the barracks. Of the original group, Bob Hosier, Art Desmond, Ben Spevack, and I were the only ones remaining together. We moved into a room across the hall. One of the occupants there, who formerly was with the 384th, had been shot down on the disastrous mission to Schweinfert to bomb the ball-bearing factory. Another, whose name I don't remember, hated the Nazis as much as did Colonel Spicer. As he killed the bedbugs in his bunk, he'd draw a picture on the side of his bed of a bug with a swastika.

The number of prisoners continued to grow, and the occupancy of the rooms increased to twenty. The halls of the barracks were lined each side with double and triple deck bunks. Barracks designed to accommodate a maximum of 120 men now housed more than 250. And it was worse in the new compound, where twenty-five men lived in a room the same size as ours. Instead of bunks, they had three tiers at each end of the room for sleeping.

*   *   *

The Red Army had swept across three hundred miles of snow-covered Poland and was momentarily halted along the Oder River. We were watching for developments around the Stettin Bay area. Something was bound to happen before long—liberation, surrender, or a much-feared forced march across territory constantly being battered and strafed by British and American bombers and fighters.

The western front was agonizingly quiet. To the impatient men cooped behind barbed wire, the quiet was disappointing. German general von Runstedt had pulled off his do-or-die push into the Ardennes, and morale at Barth had hit the skids. In February, Red Cross food parcels were cut off by the Germans, with faint hope of any more reaching us, despite the fact that the International Red Cross had more than one million parcels stored at Lubeck, the Baltic port seventy-five miles away. The Germans blamed the cut-off on the savaging of their transport facilities by the Allied strafing attacks. And, indeed, we frequently heard explosions from bursting boilers as locomotives were blown up.

The U.S. government offered to furnish Army trucks and gasoline to transport the food to the camps. Still, the Nazis seemed intent on starving us. The German food ration, not very nutritious or filling at best, was hacked to the bare minimum. Our diet consisted of a couple of potatoes, a few pieces of bread, dehydrated vegetables that no amount of boiling could tenderize, and ersatz, sugarless coffee.

We began losing weight steadily, and it became an effort to even walk outside for roll call in the freezing weather. No one said much about the effect of the diet on our physical condition, but we all knew we couldn't last very much longer on the ration. Many complained of blacking out every time they got up from their bunks. We were too weak to do anything but lie there and conserve what energy we had for the expected forced march. Several camps to the east had been moved in advance of the Russian forces moving toward Berlin and the Pomeranian area. Not only were we weakened from our near-starvation, but our feet and ankles were swollen, and we were very afraid of a march.

There were a few cats around camp, but they all disappeared as the kriegies became desperate for food. A few POWs had saved D-ration chocolate bars and sold what they dared spare for as much as twenty-five dollars apiece. Early one morning during the famine, the men from the room next to ours found a pin-tailed duck and about thirty jays that had crashed against the barracks during the night. At least they had something to eat that day.

Food became the chief topic of conversation, uppermost in the minds of all. The war was nearly forgotten.

*　*　*

A few days before my second Easter in captivity, the miracle for which we had been praying finally came to pass. A trainload of American Red Cross food parcels arrived. And they kept coming in by rail and truck until we had nearly ninety thousand of them in camp. The sudden influx of food began almost simultaneously with the Allied surge across the crumbling Reich. Morale soared like a rocket, and kriegie chefs went into action, preparing elaborate Easter dinners. To top it off, the Germans, who a few days earlier were trying to starve us, brought in tons of potatoes and cabbage to augment the Red Cross food.

Max Schmeling, former world heavyweight boxing champion, who had served in the German army as a paratrooper before being wounded in the landing on Crete, visited Stalag Luft I April 23 on a goodwill tour. The Germans, realizing that the struggle was all but over, started making overtures of friendship.

Eisenhower's forces were racing unopposed along the German autobahns.[1] Red Star bulletins on the progress of the final drive into Germany began coming in daily, then hourly.

The Russian Army had broken across the Oder River headed for Berlin, but things were still quiet along Stettin Bay, the area most critical to our situation. Every night, we listened for sounds of

1. This experience supposedly inspired Eisenhower's plans to construct the United States interstate highway system.

artillery. It was a toss-up as to who would reach us first—the Americans and British or the Russians. The only sounds were those from some leather-lunged kriegie yelling, "Come on Joe" (referring to Joseph Stalin), or "Come on Ike."

Finally, during the wee hours of an April morning, we were awakened by a faint rumble. The Russians had opened a steady barrage of artillery fire and soon were to come storming across the flat lands of Pomerania.

The war was progressing favorably, but we at Barth were still in a stew. We felt certain the Germans would never surrender nine thousand Allied prisoners and themselves to the Russians. And we weren't even certain the Russians would recognize our establishment as a prisoner of war camp for Allied airmen. They might arrive shooting and ask questions later. Our anxiety was feverish.

Then Gestapo chief Heinrich Himmler came to Stalag Luft I one day and our anxiety boiled. Himmler had moved his headquarters to the little town of Zingst, seven miles away, and it appeared that Pomerania was to be a garrison of last-ditch defense for the stubbornly dying Reich. We wondered whether he had come to camp to carry out some executions. We discovered later that he had fled to our area hoping to reach the British lines to surrender, which he did three weeks later.

At dusk on the afternoon of April 28, 1945, I was walking along the double barbed-wire fence separating our compound from the north compound when I heard someone call me. It was Colonel Zemke, standing on the other side. He looked up to the guard tower to make sure he wasn't being watched, then said, "Lieutenant, get this over to Colonel Wilson right away." After again glancing at the guard tower, he threw a Nescafé can over the fence. As directed, I delivered the message to Colonel Wilson in the barracks next to mine immediately. I surmised that Zemke was making plans to cope with whatever fate was in store for us.

We learned later that Zemke had been planning all along for the time when hostilities would cease. He had initiated the subject with the camp Kommandant von Warnstedt, telling the lager chief that a forced march out of the prison was not in the interest of either the Germans or the Allied prisoners. On a later occasion, during one of the periodic visits by a representative from a neutral country, Zemke thought this might be the time to broach the subject again. While walking outside the main gate at the suggestion of Warnstedt, Zemke suggested that, since the war was nearing its end, a plan should be drawn up to have the command of Stalag Luft I transferred from the Germans to Provisional Wing X, Zemke's name for the Allied military organization of the POWs. He asked the Swiss agent if he would be willing to help both parties in drafting such a plan. Before Warnstedt could say anything, the man from Switzerland vociferously protested, saying that the protecting power could not participate in such an agreement because it would violate its role of neutrality.

Some on the Provisional Wing X staff proposed taking control of the camp by force. Zemke was firmly against such a move, arguing that there would be loss of life and repercussions, such as giving the SS the excuse to come in and carry out mass executions. Zemke suggested letting the German camp authorities know they would be treated well if they relinquished control. This was done by preparing Provisional Wing X post regulations outlining the behavior of both the POWs and the camp administrators for when control of the camp was transferred, emphasizing there were to be no reprisals. Zemke made sure a copy would wind up in Warnstedt's possession.

Some time later Zemke was summoned to a meeting with Warnstedt, who showed him a directive he had received from his superiors. The message ordered an evacuation of all personnel at Stalag Luft I to a destination near Hamburg within twenty-four hours. After Warnstedt's staff officers unanimously agreed to ignore the evacuation order, Zemke went to see Warnstedt, who again invited him to take a walk. On that walk, he told Zemke, "Der Krieg ist jetzt uber fur uns"—The war is now over for us.

The morning after Zemke ordered me to take a message to Colonel Wilson, we were told to dig slit trenches and foxholes near our barracks for protection from bombing and strafing. Before noon the compound was a maze of mounded dirt—dug mostly with tin cans. We learned that day of the order to evacuate, which someone in the office at Zingst had rescinded. It was rumored throughout the camp that the Germans were preparing to leave. When they began blowing up equipment at the flak school that afternoon, we knew this was more than a rumor.

At roll call lager officer Cragg and a mere six guards entered the compound, counted us, then left hurriedly. It was to be our last formation. About dusk the demolitions became louder and more frequent. I saw Germans escaping into the woods with Red Cross food parcels tucked under their arms. Colonel Greening gathered volunteers to go to the storehouse at the flak school to rescue the parcels that were left. They had to fight off German soldiers and civilians who were looting the place. The Kommandant told Greening he could do nothing to stop them. Greening and his volunteers went into action and brought twenty thousand parcels to the camp in five trips.

The Russians Arrive

★   ★   ★

During the night all German personnel left, and we awoke next morning to see the Stars and Stripes flying from the compound's flagpole in place of the Nazi swastika. The flag had been sewn with scraps of red, white, and blue cloth fragments by an unknown kriegie. I am still amazed at the incomparable ingenuity and varied talents among men in such primitive surroundings. At long last we were free!

Instead of Germans, Zemke's assigned guards were patrolling the fences and manning the towers. The young and wise colonel was determined to keep us together and to maintain discipline. We may have resented being disciplined at the time, but in retrospect over the years we have come to realize the wisdom of our young colonel. I know that I do.

Zemke sent scouting parties to contact the Russians, who were reported to be just four kilometers away. The town of Barth was fully prepared for unconditional capitulation. Large red flags jutted prominently from the windows of the houses. The bürgermeister, fearing the Russians, had committed suicide. His successor promised Zemke complete cooperation.

That night, I listened to *Hit Parade* over the American Forces Network for the first time in nearly a year and a half. The barracks halls were jammed with joyful kriegies listening, too, as the program came over the loudspeaker.

The following day we listened to records of American big

bands, sounds most of us hadn't heard in a long time. Suddenly a soft opening strain gave way to the loud noise of whistles, guns, and drums in Spike Jones' inimitable arrangement of "Cocktails for Two." Kriegies lying in their bunks jumped up, startled, imagining the Russian army had arrived shooting.

Not long after, the sound of the barracks radio was drowned by a burst of cheers. A Russian advance patrol had entered the main gate—a lieutenant and a private in a German truck driven by a Frenchman just liberated from a Gestapo jail at Stralsund. While this was occurring, German radio was announcing the death of Adolf Hitler in the garrison at Berlin.

More Russians arrived next morning, and Colonel Zemke began trying to contact American headquarters to arrange our evacuation. The Russian colonel in command threw a monkey wrench into Zemke's plans, however, and told him we would march to Rostock at six that night to meet the American Ninth Army units.

While we were hurriedly preparing for the journey, the Russian colonel, a bit inebriated and in a holiday mood (it was May Day), poked a gun in Zemke's face and suggested he let the kriegies out from behind barbed wire. Before Zemke could respond, the fences were ripped down and the colonel's discipline scattered to the winds. A mad dash to the flak school, the town of Barth, everywhere, ensued.

A march to Rostock was out of the question now, but several groups of adventuresome ex-POWs were seen scattering in every direction, packs of food and clothing on their backs. Souvenir-crazed ex-kriegies tramped the area laden with boots, helmets, jackets, caps, and flight suits the Luftwaffe had stored in the big red brick buildings of the flak school.

Barth, the main attraction for the liberated men, was a scene of wild disorder. Russian soldiers, still under the effects of the May Day binge, paraded the streets in carriages, trucks, wagons, motorcycles, bicycles, every conceivable type of vehicle. Ex-kriegies, getting their first taste of freedom in months and even years, roamed everywhere, yelling *Tovarich* to each and every Russian they spotted on the streets. German civilians huddled frightened in the doorways, on the sidewalks, and in homes. Red and white flags of surrender hung from every window in town.

Sergeant Roger Armstrong, who was among a group of kriegies

evacuated from Stalag IV near Danzig, visited the cathedral in Barth, where he saw a glass case with an engraved brass plate, which described the contents of the case as a silver communion set once used by Martin Luther. Armstrong was tempted to take the case, but felt it would be wrong. Later that day he returned to the cathedral and found the glass case smashed and its precious contents gone.

The Russian commander next day imposed martial law on Barth and its vicinity. Zemke appealed to us to stay put and to obey his and the Russian orders. "They don't know you, men," he declared during an impromptu convocation. "Be careful, behave yourselves, and above all, be patient. We'll be getting out of here soon."

Confusion and anxiety at the camp spawned a number of rumors. Word was going around that the Russians planned to take us to the Black Sea port of Odessa, from where we eventually would be returned to our home nations.[1] Zemke wanted to have us flown to France, then home—a much shorter and more expeditious route.

One night as we were waiting for our evacuation to be decided, the Russians showed us a newsreel of the Yalta meeting. Those of us who had not seen photographs of FDR in a year or more were shocked to see how bad the recently deceased president had looked.[2] At a meeting with our officers, a Russian colonel said, ". . . the men in my command are all wearing black armbands in mourning the death of your great leader. And I would like your men to exhibit the same mourning." There ensued a frantic search to find black cloth, which we scavenged from a variety of sources, principally from the lining of our GI overcoats.

At the time, I don't believe any of us fully appreciated what Hubert Zemke did for the kriegies of Stalag Luft I. The son of German immigrants, Zemke could communicate effectively with our captors. He also was fluent in Russian, having worked in the U.S. embassy in Moscow. His P-47 Thunderbolt carried the name *Moy Tovarich*, My Comrade. Because of Zemke's language and leadership skills, Stalag Luft I was probably the only German POW installation not moved during those last traumatic days.

1. Years later I found out how this rumor came about. Apparently the Russian leaders in command of our situation believed Allied planes were not allowed to fly over Russian-held territory under provisions agreed upon by Roosevelt, Churchill, and Stalin at the Yalta Conference.
2. We had learned of his death a couple of weeks before our liberation.

Getting us out of Germany and out of the hands of our troublesome allies was also the result of his abilities. Zemke had sent RAF Group Captain C. T. Weir to contact British Field Marshall Bernard L. Montgomery to convince the Russians it would be impossible for the inmates of our camp to make the arduous journey to Odessa. Reportedly, Montgomery met with Marshal Rokossovsky, the commander of the white Russian army group that had overrun Berlin and all the area around the Baltic. As a result Captain Weir reported on his return that plans had been worked out to have the Eighth Air Force come to the nearby air field and evacuate Stalag Luft I.

There were many doubting Thomases in the camp, however, who didn't want to wait. They left in droves. One group commandeered a German locomotive, which was seen steaming west. Four of my roommates decided to head for Sweden. They found a small fishing boat and traveled only a short distance from the Baltic shore before the vessel sunk. They returned dripping wet and thoroughly embarrassed, deciding to await more dependable transportation home.

The majority of us made the same decision. It seemed to me most of those who left had spent the least time in captivity. Old-timers apparently figured a few more days would not make much difference. So, as Zemke advised, we waited, albeit impatiently, for the bombers of the Eighth Air Force to arrive.

The airfield, less than three miles away, was small, and Zemke was told by American authorities that the field must be inspected thoroughly before the big B-17s would be allowed to land. Work parties labored for several days removing mines and booby traps left by the fleeing Germans. Focke-Wulfs and JU-88s parked around the perimeter of the field were checked and tagged with red flags if they were suspected of being mined.

To occupy our time while the airfield was being cleared, Zemke and his Russian counterpart agreed to let small organized groups of kriegies go on walking tours of the area. We visited the airfield and saw several German planes parked about the abandoned field. Most were marked with little red flags, indicating that they had been checked and cleared of any mines or booby traps left by the fleeing Germans. I recall looking into the cockpit of a JU-88 two-engine fighter-bomber, one of the Luftwaffe's finest planes, and imagining the havoc it wreaked when it had been used as a rocket firing craft.

After touring the airfield, our group walked a mile or so south of Barth and came upon what appeared to be a prison. Like Stalag Luft I, the installation was ringed with barbed wire and guarded from watchtowers, but it also was encircled by electrified wire. Though the site was unoccupied, there lingered the unmistakable odor of death.

We later heard that several kriegies, including doctors and paramedics had driven to that camp shortly after the SS guards fled the approaching Russians, treated the few remaining survivors, cleaned the place, and buried the remains of up to three hundred prisoners. The visitors were told that the site had been a slave labor camp in which had been interned approximately fifteen hundred men and women, most of them from Germany. The inmates included political prisoners, supposed saboteurs, espionage agents, deserters, black marketeers, and other enemies of the Reich. Most of the inmates, however, were there because they were Jewish.

Those who cleaned up the installation described conditions there much as others would later describe Belsen, Dachau, Buchenwald, and Auschwitz.

German civilians, rounded up to dig mass graves for the dead prisoners, were frightened, believing the graves were intended for them. One of them said he had heard about death camps from BBC broadcasts, but had dismissed the reports as propaganda.

*   *   *

The runways were finally cleared of mines, the tower radio put in order, shipping rosters prepared, and the all clear given for some three hundred Fortresses of the first division of the Eighth Air Force to fly in and begin transporting kriegies out of Germany.

Auf Wiedersehen Deutschland

★   ★   ★

A few days after liberation, several members of the camp produced a two-page news sheet, "Barth Hard Times." A banner
headline exclaimed "RUSSKY COME!" and the dateline
read "Vol 1, No 1, Last 1, Saturday, May 5th, 1945, Price 1 D-Bar."
The editor was listed as F/L E. R. Inkpen, and chief writers were
Lowell Bennett and Nelson Giddings. The paper was printed with
some difficulty. The presses of the Barth newspaper had been taken
over, but the linotype machines had been smashed by freed slave la-
borers and the typewriters thrown out the second-floor windows.
The type, therefore, had to be set by hand. The front page featured a
black and white cartoon showing kriegies swarming a Soviet tank,
with the caption, "What D'Ye Know, Joe!!"

Group Captain Wier wrote a column titled "Relieved," which
stated:

> Colonel Zemke intended to write this appreciation for the relief
> of Stalag Luft I, but unfortunately necessary duties have made
> this impossible. He has, in his own words "taken a powder" to
> make final arrangements with the relieving Soviet forces.
>
> It is therefore my privilege to introduce this Memorial
> Edition of the BARTH HARD TIMES. During the successes,
> reverses and stagnant periods encountered during this struggle,

our newspaper has faithfully recorded the German war communiques and expanded upon them in capable editorials.

With the redemption of a continent, our exile is ended. Our barb-bound community will soon be a memory. So, on behalf of Colonel Zemke and myself, to all our fellow-kriegies: "GOOD LUCK!"

On the afternoon of May 12th, the first group of planes landed at the cleared airfield and flew some nine hundred British prisoners back to England. The following morning, we marched to the airfield.

Our evacuation was well planned, and we were more than willing to cooperate. The planes arrived in groups of about twenty, flying over in loose formation, then peeling off one by one. As a plane landed and slowly taxied approximately twenty-five men would hurriedly pile in. When all were aboard, the plane would turn and taxi into position for takeoff when the last plane of the group had landed.

The group I was in boarded a bomber about one o'clock that afternoon. I grabbed a spot near one of the waist windows so I could see Germany once more from the air. After takeoff we were headed for Laon, France, near Reims—some four hours away. We flew at an altitude of about eight thousand feet, passing over several cities, or what was left of them. Hamburg, Cologne, Essen, Rostock, Lubeck, and Hanover looked like sprawling brick yards, acres and acres of rubble. At Cologne, it seemed the only identifiable structure remaining was a big cathedral near the banks of the Rhine. Armored vehicle tracks crisscrossed the devastated landscape.

We landed at an airfield near Laon late that afternoon and were greeted by a Red Cross van dispensing coffee and doughnuts. It had been at least two years since I tasted anything so good.

GI trucks transported us to a tent camp that evening, and we were shown to a mess tent. Medical personnel there warned us to go easy on the amount of food we ate. We were mainly impressed with the GI bread—so different from the black bread we had eaten for so long.

The following morning, we boarded trucks and were taken to the railroad station in Laon for a journey to a RAMP[1] camp on the Normandy coast. Our destination was Camp Lucky Strike, a huge tent installation at Saint Valéry, between Dieppe and Fecamp.

1. Recovered Allied Military Personnel.

There were several such camps in the area, all bearing the names of American cigarettes.

Soon after departing, we reached Reims, passing by the "Little Red School House," in which the Germans had formally surrendered to General Eisenhower a few days earlier. We stopped in the station for about an hour, and some of us got off the train. When I returned and the train had left Reims, one of my friends told me a major from Supreme Headquarters Allied Expeditionary Forces had come aboard looking for me. I later discovered the major was Archie Gauthier, a neighbor from my hometown, Sunshine, Louisiana. A member of Eisenhower's staff, he knew from the travel manifest that I was on the train.

The train trip to Lucky Strike was about as slow as the earlier journey from Frankfurt to Barth. When we stopped in Rouen, many of us got off to get a drink of water from a hose outside the depot. A few hours later the train was forced to stop. We should have remembered not to drink that water.

★   ★   ★

We arrived at Saint Valéry the following afternoon and were taken to Camp Lucky Strike, a vast sea of tents, near the Normandy coast. There must have been nearly forty-five thousand ex-kriegies there. Almost immediately after arriving at the tent city, we shed our clothes, deloused, showered, then were issued new uniforms and bedding and assigned to a tent.

The next day, we began processing for the voyage home. The first order of business was a physical examination, which in my case revealed I was in relatively good health, except for being about thirty pounds underweight. I was lean, but not nearly as frail as I had been a few months earlier in Stalag Luft I.

We were then assigned to report to intelligence officers for debriefing. We were questioned about our last mission before capture, our group, target, and so forth, as well as about our treatment at the hands of our captors.

Adjacent to the array of tents was a small airfield. As soon as word got out about the ex-POWs at Lucky Strike, the field was swarmed with planes flown by men trying to locate old friends. Pop Dolan arrived from England, checking on ex-members of the

384th, and we chatted about prison life and what went on at Grafton Underwood after I was shot down.

We spent most nights at Lucky Strike watching movies in some of the larger tents. Even though it was mid-May, it turned cold at night, and we bundled up to watch the movies and even slept in our clothes.

The mess tents were manned by German POWs, with whom we heatedly argued about the size of portions they distributed to us. Medical personnel had to intervene, reminding us that after months and years of deprivation, our digestive systems couldn't accommodate the amount of food we wanted. The Germans, we were told, were only following medical orders.

I tried to locate my cousin Gerald LaPlace, who had been shot down in October. I couldn't find him, but I did track down some of my crew members who had been in Stalag XVII with Gerald. In a letter to my folks dated May 19, 1945, I wrote, ". . . three of our enlisted men have already gone home—Wolfe, Mason, and Harris. Nichols, Tucker, and Argenbright are still here. I saw Nichols yesterday morning and he told me his tale of woe and liberation. They had a rough time for a while—moved several times. The Russians were 18 miles from them last July and the Germans walked them for 86 days to another camp and then gave themselves up. Nick took a Luger and a pint of hooch off a Jerry Hauptmann (captain) in charge of them."

Lucky Strike was the strangest military establishment I had ever seen. No one seemed to be in charge. We weren't told what to expect or when we might be going home. Nothing. Impatience took hold again. On May 26, two weeks after leaving Germany, I wrote the following in a letter home, "Still hanging around waiting to ship home. I'm going to England in a few days and expect to leave from there. I should get home in 3 or 4 weeks, perhaps later. Gen. Eisenhower was here the other day to tell us he's doing all he can to get us home as soon as possible. I got a good peek at Ike—he walks amongst the crowd and chats with the men—informal as hell—a genuine personality."

General Eisenhower apparently got word of the situation at Lucky Strike when one of his aides called his attention to an article in *Stars and Stripes*. The article described conditions at the huge installation, such as overcrowding, lack of sanitation, malnutrition and a general mood of discontent. Disturbed by the report, Eisenhower decided to have a firsthand look. Several U.S. senators who had come to Europe to assess postwar conditions were in the offices of the Supreme Headquarters of the Allied Expeditionary Forces in London to meet with General Eisenhower, and he invited them along, telling them that at no other place would they have an opportunity to see so many citizens of the United States.

Word of the general's appearance at Lucky Strike spread like wildfire. He and his entourage were followed everywhere by an ecstatic, cheering horde. I was at hand when the commander emerged from a mess tent, and he shook hands with several of us. Among the five senators accompanying Ike, I recognized Burton K. Wheeler of Montana, the Senate's leading isolationist; Homer Capehart, Indiana; and Henry Hickenlooper, Iowa.

A resourceful group of ex-POWs located a GI truck and a sound system, which they set up, and persuaded the general to say a few words before he headed back to London. As Ike climbed up to the back of the truck, a tremendous roar erupted. Ike took hold of the microphone, raised his other hand, and waited for the cheering to subside. Then he grinned and said, "Hold on, fellas, I'm not a movie star—just another GI!"

He told us he was aware of two main complaints cited in the newspaper article. About the food, he said he and the senators agreed the chow was bland and tasteless, but reminded us that the doctors were concerned about our digestive systems. "I don't want to challenge the doctors on this matter," he said. "They're only doing what's best for all of you."

As for our impatience and frustration about getting back home, Ike reminded us that we were still at war with Japan and shipping was at a premium. "I appreciate your concern and anxiety," he said, "but please be patient with us."

Despite Ike's plea for patience, unrest at Lucky Strike prevailed. We felt penned up and were as anxious as ever to get moving—somewhere. Many ex-kriegies decided to leave the tent city, and most of those headed for Paris, less than a hundred miles away.

I still hadn't been able to find Britt and Haley, and I figured they had either already been shipped home or had left for Paris or England. I decided then that England might be the best point for my departure home.

Sixteen

Heading Home

Oone of the pilots from the 384th flew in to Lucky Strike a few days later, and I hitched a ride with him back to Grafton Underwood. I hardly recognized the place. It was spring, and in place of the snow and mud I had known, there was an abundance of green grass and wildflowers. The only personnel I knew were a few of the ground officers.

I spent the night in my former barracks. After breakfast I went to Kettering, where I took a train to London. Americans in uniform rode free. After arriving at Victoria Station I sought a place to stay and found quarters at a place called the Reindeer Club, a Red Cross facility near Piccadilly. The following day I went to the Allied headquarters offices and received a partial payment of back pay due. One of the officers there had been a navigator in the 384th who bunked next to me at Grafton Underwood.

I met Britt and Haley at the Grosvenor Square dining hall one day.[1] I hadn't seen them since I was moved to another compound in the prison camp about a year earlier. They seemed to be enjoying their stay in London.

Another day a couple of us staying at the Reindeer Club took a walking tour of London, escorted by a retired major from the British army, who took us to see just about every historical sight to

1. Grosvenor Square housed the headquarters of SHAEF and the American Embassy. The GIs called it Eisenhowerplatz.

see in London—Westminster Abbey, the Tower of London, Ten Downing Street, Buckingham Palace, Hyde Park, and Saint Paul's Cathedral. My ankles swelled so much I could hardly remove my shoes.

I also spent time seeing a few theatrical performances and movies and visiting the shopping district. At Harrod's, I purchased a new uniform and had a tailor on Bond Street convert the coat into a battle jacket, a style copied from the RAF, also referred to as an Eisenhower jacket.

Sam Walker, one of the original members of the Spider Kelly gang at Barth, was also staying at the Reindeer Club. He told me he had dated an American girl named Kennedy whose father had been the ambassador to England. After two weeks in London, Sam and I and a couple other friends decided we needed to do something about getting home, so we went to the American embassy and voiced our impatience. In a couple days we were on a bus to Salisbury. After staying a day or two there in what appeared to have been a boy's academy, we wound up on a train to Plymouth, where we boarded an LST convoy. This was about the middle of June. Sam and I got on the same LST and were quartered with one of the ship's officers. The only other officers aboard were those from two PT boats, which were strapped to the deck. The officers of the two boats were all ex–football players from Mississippi State, UCLA, and another university.

Except for some queasiness caused by the motion of the ship, the trip was pleasant. We spent most of our time in the large cabin room eating, playing bridge, and talking about our war experiences. We also enjoyed watching the porpoises alongside the ship,

At one point the convoy halted in the middle of the Atlantic to transfer an ill passenger from one of the smaller LCIs so he could receive medical attention. A couple of days later we had to change course to dodge a hurricane that was hammering Bermuda.

After three weeks on the Atlantic, one night we sighted the distant lights on Virginia Beach. As we neared the shore near Hampton Roads next morning, a small boat joined the convoy to guide us through the harbor, which was still infested with mines placed to defend the installation.

We landed at Norfolk July 4. It was great to be on American soil once again, but the heat and humidity dampened our homecoming.

We were dressed in wool uniforms—comfortable in England, but intolerable here. As soon as we arrived at nearby Camp Patrick Henry, we obtained summer khakis at the PX.

We spent a great deal of our time there in the shower, trying to cool off while awaiting rail transportation. Sam and I headed south, by way of Cincinnati, eventually arriving at Camp Shelby in Hattiesburg, Mississippi, not far from Sam's hometown of Brookhaven. After I completed some paperwork and received a check for the rest of my back pay, I bade farewell to Sam and caught a Greyhound bus to New Orleans, where I transferred to another bus headed for Baton Rouge.

My mother, father, and grandmother were awaiting my arrival at the station. After an emotional, tearful meeting we headed for Sunshine. Home at last!

Epilogue

★　★　★

Over the years some historians have become critical of the aerial assault on Germany. One of these was fellow kriegie Lowell Bennett, the war correspondent who was shot down while flying on an RAF mission. In his book, *Parachute to Berlin*, he wrote, "My sincere conviction is that a serious strategical mistake was made in trying to bomb Germany out of the war by destroying her cities . . ."[1]

Some German leaders thought otherwise. Finance Minister Hjalmar Schact said, "Your bombers destroyed German production." General Major Herhudt von Ruden said the invasion of Europe "would have been impossible without strategic bombing." Generals Kesselring and von Runstedt agreed that, in Kesselring's words, "Allied airpower was the greatest single reason for the German defeat." And Hermann Goering, chief of the Luftwaffe, declared shortly before he committed suicide in 1945, "Without the United States Air Force the war would still be going on . . . and not on German soil."

The U.S. Army Air Force received numerous compliments, but the greatest was from Winston Churchill: "They never flinched

---

1. Later in his text, Bennett explains that he was referring to the RAF in his criticism. He pointed out that the U.S. strategic bombing policy was aimed at the destruction of specific installations—aircraft assembly plants, transportation centers, ball bearing factories, submarine pens, refineries, munitions factories, etc., not cities, as was the aim of the Royal Air Force.

or failed. It is to their devotion that in no small measure we owe our victory."

I remain convinced that the bombing of Germany was a major factor in its defeat. We did not ". . . try to bomb Germany out of the war by destroying her cities . . ." as Bennett claims, however. The Allies did not expect strategic bombing to do the entire job. It takes ground troops, tactical air power, and seapower to bring such a foe to unconditional surrender.

★ ★ ★

The day of my entry into combat, January 7, 1944, was also the day the Eighth Air Force was put in the command of General Jimmy Doolittle.

This was also the time when the P-51 Mustang joined the air war over Europe. The Mustang was the only U.S. plane originally designed during World War II. During its early testing, its Allison engine was found to be insufficient for high-altitude or long-range flights, and the plane was reequipped with the British Rolls Royce Merlin engine, which vastly improved its performance.

At the same time, Doolittle ordered a major change in the policy of the Eighth. It is said that when he visited one of the fighter bases he saw a sign in the headquarters' office, which stated that the sole responsibility of the fighter plane was to protect the bombers, or words to that effect. Doolittle said, "Take that sign down. Right now. From now on fighters will be expected to do more. Our purpose will be to destroy the Luftwaffe not only in the air but also on the ground." Thus a rejuvenated tactical mission to support the strategic bombing effort was put into effect. Involving the long-range P-51 allowed the air force not only in to wrest control of the air from the Luftwaffe, but also to strafe transportation facilities and German air bases after the bombers had been escorted to their strategic targets. Beginning in the early spring of 1944, the bombers had a much easier time carrying out their missions, to the point where General Eisenhower could assure Allied troops on D-Day that ". . . the only planes you will see overhead will be ours."

★ ★ ★

I look back on my days in World War II with mixed emotion. At the time I'm sure I must have shared the feeling of immortality that most young people feel, an outlook that no doubt resulted in so few air crew members requesting transfer to some other duty.[2]

At the time I flew, a tour of duty was twenty-five missions (later raised to thirty, then thirty-five). We knew the odds were against completing a tour of duty because so few crews had. Reportedly the first to do so was the crew of the *Memphis Belle*. The *Belle's* group, the Ninety-first, was formed in Baton Rouge at Harding Field on April 15, 1942, a couple of weeks before I entered the Army Air Corps. Not until years later did I learn how steep those odds had really been.

In an earlier chapter I mentioned the chivalry the Luftwaffe exhibited toward enemy airmen and related an incident that resulted in a meeting years later between a German and an American pilot. This so-called code of the air worked the other way too. In October 1943, a pilot of a bomber from the One-hundredth violated the code on a mission to Regensburg. His plane had suffered major damage and lagged in the formation. Several German fighters closed in on the stricken straggler, then the B-17 pilot lowered his landing gear. This was considered to be a signal of surrender, so the Luftwaffe fighters refrained from attack. The American pilot apparently changed his mind and retracted the landing gear as the Fortress gunners began blasting at the German planes, downing several of them as the B-17 dashed toward England. It didn't make it. The enraged German fliers moved in and shot the bomber down in a matter of minutes.

From then on that group was known throughout the Eighth Air Force as the Bloody One-hundreth, because the Luftwaffe concentrated on their planes, clearly marked with a square D on their tails. In subsequent missions, the One-hundreth suffered disproportionate losses; on some only one or two of the group's planes returned to base.

I've often wondered what might have happened if we had been able to get back to England on that fateful Friday. Would we have been blown to bits on the next raid? Would we have completed our

2. All air crew service was voluntary, so such a request would be granted with no resulting bad mark on the applicant's record.

tour of duty, or would we have eventually been shot down and killed by irate German citizens? I don't know, but I do know I can look back, thankful for having been among the survivors and proud of having contributed to relegating the evils of Nazism to what Professor Ambrose calls "the ashcan of history."

Afterword

★ ★ ★

he basis of the foregoing memoirs was a hurriedly written account of my prisoner-of-war experiences that I put together from memory and a few notes as soon as I returned home from England in July 1945. It was soon put away and forgotten. Like my contemporaries, I was too busy reestablishing my life—finding a job, getting married, starting a family, buying a home, meeting mortgage payments; a myriad of distractions from the nightmare of war. Only in recent years, as our generation settled into retirement and was exposed to publicity about anniversaries of the events of the 1940s, have we begun to reminisce.

Early in 1995, I was reminded of how long we had put aside those memories. I had written an article for the *Ex POW Bulletin*, "Hubert Zemke—A Man to Remember." I received a number of phone calls and letters from ex-kriegies around the country. Jim Gohlson, residing in a retirement community in Arizona, wrote to inform me he not only had been in the same compound in Stalag Luft I for fifteen months, but he also had lived less than a block away from me on the same street in Baton Rouge for twenty-two years before moving to Arizona. We had been neighbors for more than two decades and had both worked at Louisiana State University, but neither of us knew the other had been a prisoner of war.

I recently learned of a similar story even closer to home. Harry Abboud, who lived adjacent to the home behind us, had also been a

POW, incarcerated in Stalag Luft III. Harry, who died a year before I discovered this fact, had been a navigator on a B-24 Liberator in the Fifteenth Air Force located in Foggia, Italy. On one of the missions targeting the oil refineries in Ploesti, Romania, in the early fall of 1944, his plane was hit over Yugoslavia and he was captured. His brother-in-law, Bill Lignos, said Harry didn't say much about his experience, but did tell him that the Yugoslavs "were pretty mean."

About six years ago, Joe Dale, former commandant of cadets in the ROTC program at LSU and fellow member of the class of 1942, gave me a copy of a retired officers' magazine with a story about General Jimmy Doolittle. After reading it another brief item caught my eye, an article about the Escape and Evasion Society, a group of ex-airmen who had eluded capture after being shot down in enemy territory.

I wrote to the society asking if they knew the whereabouts of Ernie Lindell, whom I had not seen nor heard from since we had been shot down in 1944. They gave me Ernie's address and phone number, and I called his home in Moses Lake, Washington. After he recovered from the shock of hearing a voice from the past, we had a long conversation. He told me that the 384th Bomb Group was having its fiftieth anniversary reunion in Irvine, California, in October and urged me to attend.

I then wrote to Ralph Haley in Denver and to his sister in-law, Dorothy (his twin brother's widow), inviting them to join the Richards and the Lindells in Irvine. None of us had ever been to such a reunion. A few months later I saw Ben Spevack's name published in the membership list of the *Ex POW Bulletin*, and contacted him. He had just moved from Brooklyn to Los Angeles. Though he was not a member of the 384th, he said he would join us.

The reunion had prompted me to dig out the account of my prisoner-of-war days and rewrite it. I gave each of them copies when we met in Irvine. I have since expanded it further.

Before the reunion, Ernie sent me a copy of a cryptic diary of his evasion from his would-be captors. It told of his hiding behind a haystack and seeing our plane crashing into a nearby house, wiping out a flak battery emplacement. He ran into a wooded area and met a farmer, who took him to his house and bandaged his wounded arm. Ernie slept in a barn that night during an RAF bombing attack.

Ernie managed to elude the Germans and made his way to Amiens, where he was assisted by the French Resistance Forces. He stayed in a home there for three months "... reading, learning a little French, helping kids with English and algebra lessons, playing black jack, poker, pinochle, etc. ..."

The Resistance helped move him farther south in the late spring 1944 and eventually over the Pyrenees Mountains to Spain. He reached Madrid on June 4 and on D-Day, June 6, arrived at the Rock of Gibralter. The next day he left for England, in time to experience some bombardment of London by the buzz bombs, whose launching sites we had hit six months before on that fateful mission. He arrived in Washington, D.C., on July 1.

At the reunion Ernie said he and his wife, Connie, had attended a get-together of the Escape and Evasion Society in Savannah, Georgia, the year before. Several of the French and Belgians who had helped downed Allied airmen elude capture were in attendance. He said that for many years those who had been aided were sworn to secrecy.

Ernie is the only living member of our bomber crew I am in touch with now. I had visited Ray Haley and Neil Britt many years ago, before they died, and had corresponded with Ray over the years. Conway Nichols was killed in a traffic accident in Birmingham within a year after his return home from Europe. The only other crew member whose address was available from the 384th historian was Clarence Wolfe. I wrote to him before the reunion, but received no reply.

A few years earlier, I experienced a vastly different kind of reunion. A history professor at the University of Southwestern Louisiana was working on a book about German prisoners of war who had spent their captivity in Louisiana. He spent time in Germany interviewing men who had been there and persuaded about twenty of them to return for a visit. One of their stops was in Baton Rouge. The Red Stick chapter of the American Ex-POWs organization arranged a get-together in downtown Baton Rouge.

Each of us was called upon to give his name, mention his branch of service, and relate the circumstances of his capture. Most of the Americans had served in the air force, but there were some who had been in the Pacific area of operations. Nearly all the Germans had been in the Afrika Korps under the command of General Erwin Rommel. The unusual gathering was covered by the media, including an NBC crew, which followed the ex-POWs from Germany on a tour of their sites of incarceration.

The only other reunion I attended was the 51st Annual Convention of the American Ex-POWs in Baton Rouge in October 1998. About one thousand persons attended, including spouses, widows, and children of former prisoners of war.

Another event that should be related here occurred on the LSU campus in the fall of 1963. A week-long symposium on the U.S. space program was held at the university. The program featured talks by several officials from NASA, and the concluding session was a banquet at which Werner von Braun, director of the George C. Marshall Space Flight Center at Huntsville, Alabama, was scheduled to speak. My wife and I had planned to attend, and I was looking forward to meeting Braun because he had been the designer of Germany's V-1 and V-2 weapons and I had been shot down while bombing the V-1 launching sites in France some twenty years earlier. The banquet was scheduled for November 22—the day President John F. Kennedy was assassinated in Dallas. The symposium, of course, abruptly ended, and I never got the chance to meet Braun, who departed immediately.

★   ★   ★

But I've recently unearthed other ex-POW connections. My daughter and son-in-law, Kathleen and John Broussard, signed up to run in the Dublin, Ireland, City Marathon October 26, 1998, conducted by the Arthritis Foundation. Each had to raise $3,500 in contributions. After giving Kathleen a donation, we received a fund-raising letter from Melodee Spevack, daughter of my kriegie friend Ben Spevack, who would also be running in the marathon. Kathleen had also sent a letter to Art Desmond in Boston asking for a contribution. He did so and called to tell me that one of his seven sons was living in Dublin. He gave me his address, e-mail address, and phone number. And thus three offspring of the Spider Kelly Gang met near where the Eighth Air Force bomber bases were situated many years ago.

A couple days before Kathleen and John left for Ireland, I was at the 51st Annual Reunion of the American Ex-POWs in Baton Rouge and noticed a man with an LSU cap on and wearing a name tag indicating he had been in Stalag Luft I. I asked if he was from Baton Rouge since he was wearing an LSU cap. "No," he replied, "I'm from Lake Providence, but I've children who went to LSU."

We chatted briefly, exchanging tales of our war experiences, planes we had flown in combat and our remembrances of prison camp. He told me that he was a P-51 fighter pilot, knew Hubert Zemke and "Gabby" Gabreski, and that he was shot down on one of the missions to Berlin a couple of months after I was. He said he had returned to Germany a few years ago and went to Barth to look over the old POW homestead. "There's nothing there. I couldn't even find a strand of barbed wire," he said. "But some kriegies had been back before me and had planted some trees as a memorial, and I did too," he added.

Our conversation then switched to the present day and he told me his daughter was a judge in the Family Court in Baton Rouge— Toni Higginbotham. "Well, I'll be damned," I said. "My daughter is an attorney and works for Judge Higginbotham and other judges in the Family Court." I told him that I had met Toni when she conducted the ceremony at the wedding of Kathleen and John.

*　　*　　*

Earlier during the convention, I met another "alumnus" from the institution at Barth, Germany. He had grown up in Pointe Coupee Parish, Louisiana, and said that after the war he had served in the Postal Service and had retired some years ago as postmaster at Westwego, Louisiana. I told him my mother had served as post-master at Sunshine for many years. He looked at my name tag and said: "Abigail Richard. Sure I knew her. I've seen her at lots of post-masters' conventions."

Appendix

★　　★　　★

The following pages are brief notes written by Ernie Lindell after his ordeal of evading capture with the help of the French Resistance forces.[1] Ernie was the only one of our ten-man crew who didn't spend time in a prisoner of war camp.

★　　★　　★

Jan. 14 Target V Bombs 12000 ft. flak 3&4 out can't feather – tear off wing – 180° turn – out of formation losing alt falling back – flak again – Sudden pain in arm – Nav. to pilot another p.h. – Bombs away – Bail out – chute opens second time – pray and remember – wave at others & count chutes 10 yes all here. Plane circles and misses all of us. See Eng from chute – try to drift away from water. Land – 2 hay stacks & house – try to hide chute in hay. Someone shooting at me – House AA positions – Plane coming toward me to crash. Frozen to spot so pray – Plane hits house & plows up AA position – forget chute – start running – remember Mae West – discard it & run toward woods – More bombers & AA – woods full of Jerrys – AC across field. Meet farmer – Americano – parachute etc.

★　　★　　★

---

1. The notes are transcribed as written and unedited.

Hide till dark – See Jerry looking for us – farmer takes me to house – food – bandage arm, etc. Can't speak. Then English man comes – promises clothes food – no other help too many Jerrys – sleep in barn – Eng come over at nite AA opens up next door – scared and shaking – get control – just like nightmare

* * *

Jan. 15 – 44 Morning – clothes – bed – more food & depart. Meet kid – he knows I am not french – gives me 10 franks – 100 escape kit – kid diverts me – Jerry watching bridge – scared – walk past get hope. Walk all day – man asks something snub him – can't speak french – pass through 4 villages – more Jerrys – ask farmer for help – he's scared – move on – Hit Amiens sit in park – first french latrine – what a laugh – more walking – tired hungry – Ask help again – no luck – Ask help at farm – go to house – get food & arm fixed arm turned blue. Sleep in hay stack – meet people – kids lovely – old man sick – french cops – scare me – Jerry comes for food – Eat good – they check papers AGO – dog tags

* * *

15th Bring me paper See paper – all captured thats me leave that night in truck – Meet Madam Vignon 18th Say I will be back in England in 30 days – Feel good – good food – bed etc./ Meet lots of people – Mesairu D – French cop etc – they bring food Get to Madam's 17th evening Time passes – do not leave – learn a little french – read plenty of books think of home – Meet her family – help kids with Eng & algebra lessons – hear lots of storys – go out by boat – plane – Switzerland Never any mention of Spain – More Yanks and English come – couple of french one arm man American last war etc. – more stories – play black jack, poker, pinochle read think – 13 of us now – Incendiary bombs dropped on house – tin foil to fool radar – tell french what it is for – build model planes – more air raids – lose a couple of windows – see snap shots of damage – wonder about invasion – time passes – sleep late 2 boys get tired so leave – Jerry catches them – decide to stay ourselves – Chinese boy with us – finally 3 boys leave by boat they say I will be in next bunch

– That was April – Man came to see about us – trains blown up – delayed – finally leave on 17 April – just 3 months I have been in house

*   *   *

17th April 44 – Leave early morning train – follow man to depot – help lady with baby carriage – almost get lost – follow & crowd onto train – Jerry all over hell but no papers checked – train finally departs – Station well bombed – meet more Yanks on train – one from my old group a Sgt. Go thru other bombed stations and all were well bombed – figure invasion should be soon because of all bombed stations – Get to Paris station follow man – follow another man – then girl – ride subway change twice, never speak – Lots of Jerrys & pretty french women no trouble so far – Go to Gabby's house – a french cop – five of us there – Big party – champagne wine etc – almost drunk – one boy leaves – 4 sleep there.

*   *   *

18th April Go to another cop's house – nice wife & daughter good egg – Big air raid that nite – but rr yards & some bombs missed – Knocked out windows – hole in roof at foot of bed – sleep with cop – next day go for promenade See bombed area – still have US uniform under other clothes – Thursday 20th more bombs – 72 hour delayed action – more people killed – scared shake teeth knees rattle, etc. Can't go to air raid shelter – must stay in apartment – Dentist comes to see me – speaks Eng – asked about bombing, I try & explain – people pretty mad – c este la guerre Good food – all black market – get tobacco found a pipe Go to bar for wine – Gabby visits another promenade – more wine side walk cafe – see Doc again Drink too much – finally morning of 28th comes

*   *   *

28th April and Gabby comes for me – Going to leave every one says etc – Back to Gabby's – get hair cut food meet rest of gang – take subway – follow gal – get to park – follow young man – catch local train out of town – rails bombed – Get to station – can't get on train

– more Jerrys arrogant as hell – jump fence get on train and wait. Train leaves about 8 off at last this time for southern france – get in between cars – train packed – train stops – air raid – all clear – no talking all this time – Finally get a compartment – 2 french kids – one gal about 6 of us.

* * *

20th April Finally get to station get off – go to park spend part of day – eat etc lots of Jerrys Gestapo – take local train to Tuluse – wait in station 4 hrs – lots of Jerrys – ask us for match – Finally catch other train – it is also loaded but is a local & every time it stops someone gets out finally get seats – French man keep watching us lots of French Vichy cops – French seem to know what we are or they think we are German – try to make conversation no dice Finally get to late at night – Jerrys & Vichy cops every where – struggle through ticket taker get to park across street – follow man – boy does he walk fast – go through park – stumble over Jerry's legs as he sits on bench with French gal – he curses – we go on – black as hell – finally get to house – Eat – sleep – next day we are to rest – and go on

* * *

May 1 News that Jerry will be after us on 1 May so don't go – lucky because they picked up plenty of French – man was Belgian – 1 daughter 1 son & 2 twin boys – well to do – well educated – spoke English very well – heard that some of other boys before us – 1 captured at station Showed us his home in Belgium etc

* * *

3rd May Follow man – meet gal in grey and follow her – go to apt – she is American – other is Eng – have tea & American cig – L.S. we get package of LS and show her my Army uniform – she had not seen one in long time thrilled – caught bus – rode long time – driver was with underground – finally get off – walked 4 mile got in car drove away – got out of car & waited – man met us we followed

– long hard walk – finally to a barn on side of mt. we ate some of our food – slept in cow manure

* * *

4th May Dept in evening – met others from Amiens and really started across pyrnees mts – 18 of us 5 French – 3 Eng rest Americans – long hard walk very tired – slept on side of mt – gave bread tickets to one man – guess he kept them all

* * *

5th May Had little sleep last night – rain – no food – little food today tired before we started – leave at dusk new guide – walk all nite very tired crawl part of way – help carry others – food nervous hand shakes no can eat for 45 minutes – more rain – sleep very good in barn on side of mt. thought about bread tickets

* * *

6th May More food – potatoes & bread – but good – start at noon with new guide – last lap – talk about getting home – hot dogs hamburgers ice cream etc – walk until 4 in morn – carry couple of boys – finally on the top & below is spain – holler like hell – forget about Jerry & dogs in mts – French kids play in snow have wild time. Then the descent. Lost both heels to shoes slide all the time. Finally get to bottom guide leaves after telling us to follow stream – raining like hell – all wet tired dirty but happy – this was early morn 7th May 44 free at last after almost 4 months of anxiety. Part of us started to follow trail that nite – too dark can see fall in river but don't give a damn – others stay in sheppard's hut – we find other hut farther down stream – break in through roof Start fire – dry clothes & try to sleep – too tired so just talk

* * *

7th May Finally morning – no food but who cares – others catch us but the 3 french lads made in the nite before – we walk in mud &

water 4 hrs to a road & are met by Spanish cops they hold us take cig lighter – knives, etc. March us to town Old man and son give us some bread – small village – Military boy questions us – march to another town in rain singing – we are happy – free – but what a bunch of tramps – sleep in a barn by stream after some potato soup furnished by Red Cross.

* * *

8th May Really in spain my birthday – more soup – take bus to Pavyuslava – with guards of course – police station – finger prints photos etc – wait until about 2130 – cop takes us out – lights every where – first lights in 4½ – months – Hotel – friend – dinner – wine party etc. Sick

* * *

9 May Bath shave new clothes lots of good food – money to spend – wine sight seeing etc. sight seeing – GI every some tim dept 28th for Ahlowa

* * *

29th Ahlowa – swim – hike – fresh fruit – etc sun bath – drink champagne meet more men – mostly Yanks

* * *

4th June Down to Madrid – big meal – drive through town – insult German Embassy leave for Gib that nite – whole car for us on train

* * *

5 June Reach rock – customs formality they waste time finally get to Rock – physical exams – food – clothes now back in uniform. Check on other men that got through – plenty from my group.

* * *

6 June D Day 5 extras everyone happy – meet buddy from Vancouver Wash Buy cig lighter get paid. British interrogation.

* * *

7 June Dept by plane Back in Eng 8th June

* * *

8 June Back in Eng – Give bananas to Limmies they went crazy

* * *

9 June Identified interrogated etc – go to wide wing more trouble with details – physical etc. Get paid send some home

* * *

14 June 5 months to day & hr back to base – place all changed – silver ships – all new faces – couple of old buddies

* * *

17 June Back to London – more buzz bombs they started 13th Stay in Jules Club – lots of fun – met some old buddies etc. Good to be free

* * *

26 June Now 1st Lt. More waiting dept finally on 30 June

* * *

1 July Wash DC Good old USA.
Hot dogs – pie & ice cream – hamburgers
Boy its good to be home –

Sources and Acknowledgments

★ ★ ★

Information I used in writing this book came from the following sources:

★ ★ ★

My own recollection of aerial combat and of life in Stalag Luft I, which I wrote in a brief diary soon after my return home from Europe in July 1945.

★ ★ ★

Conversations and correspondence with former kriegies and others familiar with the European theater of operations during World War II. These include Art Desmond, Ben Spevack, Ralph and Ray Haley, Neil Britt, Conway Nichols, Ernest V. Lindell, John E. Welles, Joe Dale, Archie Gauthier, Gerald LaPlace, Pop Dolan, Jim Gohlson, Marion Bahlinger, Bill Lignos, Bert McDowell, Cecil Manning, Mozart Kaufman, Lloyd Carville, Don Warren, Jimmy Daigle, and Duke Hartsfield.

★ ★ ★

Mission reports from the 384th Bomb Group, letters my mother had saved for me, several magazine and newspaper stories, and a number of books relating to the air war over Europe: *Crossbow and Overcast* by James McGovern, *Zemke's Stalag* by Hubert Zemke as told to Roger Freeman, *The Mighty Eighth* by Roger Freeman, *My War* by Andy Rooney, *One Last Look* by Phillip Kaplan and Rex Smith, *U.S. The Hard Way* by Roger Armstrong, *The Lady* by Dan Patterson, *Stalag Luft III* by Arthur Durand, *Parachute to Berlin* by Lowell Bennet, *Winged Victory* by Geoffrey Perret, *First of the Many* by John (Tex) McCrary and David Scheurman, *As Briefed* by Walter Owens, and *Fall of Fortresses* by Elmer Bendiner.

*　*　*

I am especially grateful to my wife, Billie, our son Reed, our four daughters and their husbands, Kathleen Callaghan and John Broussard, Linda and Chris Abadie, Kelly and James Brown, and Donna and Mick Rainone, all of whom have shown great interest and encouragement in the project; Maradee Cryer, former coworker in what is now the LSU Office of University Relations who produced the maps of the ETO and the 384th bomber base; Barbara Yablonsky; and Bob Felton for his interest and help in compiling the several drafts of the manuscript, along with Chris Abadie and Reed Richard.

I also thank all the members of the LSU Press staff for their interest, expertise, and advice, especially Maureen Hewitt, associate director and editor in chief; John Easterly, executive editor; and Jean C. Lee, who edited *Kriegie*.